Magna Carta
and the
Disorganized Constitution
of the
United Kingdom
of·
Great Britain

EAST INDIA
PUBLISHING COMPANY
PREMIER CLASSICS

Published by the East India Publishing Company
Ottawa, Ontario.

© 2020 East India Publishing Company

Cover Design by EIPC. © 2020
9781774261927

CONTENTS

The Magna Carta

Preamble:

John, by the grace of God, king of England, lord of Ireland, duke of Normandy and Aquitaine, and count of Anjou, to the archbishop, bishops, abbots, earls, barons, justiciaries, foresters, sheriffs, stewards, servants, and to all his bailiffs and liege subjects, greetings. Know that, having regard to God and for the salvation of our soul, and those of all our ancestors and heirs, and unto the honor of God and the advancement of his holy Church and for the rectifying of our realm, we have granted as underwritten by advice of our venerable fathers, Stephen, archbishop of Canterbury, primate of all England and cardinal of the holy Roman Church, Henry, archbishop of Dublin, William of London, Peter of Winchester, Jocelyn of Bath and Glastonbury, Hugh of Lincoln, Walter of Worcester, William of Coventry, Benedict of Rochester, bishops; of Master Pandulf, subdeacon and member of the household of our lord the Pope, of brother Aymeric (master of the Knights of the Temple in England), and of the illustrious men William Marshal, earl of Pembroke, William, earl of Salisbury, William, earl of Warenne, William, earl of Arundel, Alan of Galloway (constable of Scotland), Waren Fitz Gerold, Peter Fitz Herbert, Hubert De Burgh (seneschal of Poitou), Hugh de Neville, Matthew Fitz Herbert, Thomas Basset, Alan Basset, Philip d'Aubigny, Robert of Roppesley, John Marshal, John Fitz Hugh, and others, our liegemen.

1. In the first place we have granted to God, and by this our present charter confirmed for us and our heirs

forever that the English Church shall be free, and shall have her rights entire, and her liberties inviolate; and we will that it be thus observed; which is apparent from this that the freedom of elections, which is reckoned most important and very essential to the English Church, we, of our pure and unconstrained will, did grant, and did by our charter confirm and did obtain the ratification of the same from our lord, Pope Innocent III, before the quarrel arose between us and our barons: and this we will observe, and our will is that it be observed in good faith by our heirs forever. We have also granted to all freemen of our kingdom, for us and our heirs forever, all the underwritten liberties, to be had and held by them and their heirs, of us and our heirs forever.

2. If any of our earls or barons, or others holding of us in chief by military service shall have died, and at the time of his death his heir shall be full of age and owe "relief", he shall have his inheritance by the old relief, to wit, the heir or heirs of an earl, for the whole baroncy of an earl by L100; the heir or heirs of a baron, L100 for a whole barony; the heir or heirs of a knight, 100s, at most, and whoever owes less let him give less, according to the ancient custom of fees.

3. If, however, the heir of any one of the aforesaid has been under age and in wardship, let him have his inheritance without relief and without fine when he comes of age.

4. The guardian of the land of an heir who is thus under age, shall take from the land of the heir nothing but reasonable produce, reasonable customs, and reasonable services, and that without destruction or waste of men or goods; and if we have committed the wardship of the lands of any such minor to the sheriff, or to any other who is responsible to us for its issues, and he has made

destruction or waster of what he holds in wardship, we will take of him amends, and the land shall be committed to two lawful and discreet men of that fee, who shall be responsible for the issues to us or to him to whom we shall assign them; and if we have given or sold the wardship of any such land to anyone and he has therein made destruction or waste, he shall lose that wardship, and it shall be transferred to two lawful and discreet men of that fief, who shall be responsible to us in like manner as aforesaid.

5. The guardian, moreover, so long as he has the wardship of the land, shall keep up the houses, parks, fishponds, stanks, mills, and other things pertaining to the land, out of the issues of the same land; and he shall restore to the heir, when he has come to full age, all his land, stocked with ploughs and wainage, according as the season of husbandry shall require, and the issues of the land can reasonable bear.

6. Heirs shall be married without disparagement, yet so that before the marriage takes place the nearest in blood to that heir shall have notice.

7. A widow, after the death of her husband, shall forthwith and without difficulty have her marriage portion and inheritance; nor shall she give anything for her dower, or for her marriage portion, or for the inheritance which her husband and she held on the day of the death of that husband; and she may remain in the house of her husband for forty days after his death, within which time her dower shall be assigned to her.

8. No widow shall be compelled to marry, so long as she prefers to live without a husband; provided always that she gives security not to marry without our consent,

if she holds of us, or without the consent of the lord of whom she holds, if she holds of another.

9. Neither we nor our bailiffs will seize any land or rent for any debt, as long as the chattels of the debtor are sufficient to repay the debt; nor shall the sureties of the debtor be distrained so long as the principal debtor is able to satisfy the debt; and if the principal debtor shall fail to pay the debt, having nothing wherewith to pay it, then the sureties shall answer for the debt; and let them have the lands and rents of the debtor, if they desire them, until they are indemnified for the debt which they have paid for him, unless the principal debtor can show proof that he is discharged thereof as against the said sureties.

10. If one who has borrowed from the Jews any sum, great or small, die before that loan be repaid, the debt shall not bear interest while the heir is under age, of whomsoever he may hold; and if the debt fall into our hands, we will not take anything except the principal sum contained in the bond.

11. And if anyone die indebted to the Jews, his wife shall have her dower and pay nothing of that debt; and if any children of the deceased are left under age, necessaries shall be provided for them in keeping with the holding of the deceased; and out of the residue the debt shall be paid, reserving, however, service due to feudal lords; in like manner let it be done touching debts due to others than Jews.

12. No scutage not aid shall be imposed on our kingdom, unless by common counsel of our kingdom, except for ransoming our person, for making our eldest son a knight, and for once marrying our eldest daughter; and for these there shall not be levied more than a reasonable

aid. In like manner it shall be done concerning aids from the city of London.

13. And the city of London shall have all it ancient liberties and free customs, as well by land as by water; furthermore, we decree and grant that all other cities, boroughs, towns, and ports shall have all their liberties and free customs.

14. And for obtaining the common counsel of the kingdom anent the assessing of an aid (except in the three cases aforesaid) or of a scutage, we will cause to be summoned the archbishops, bishops, abbots, earls, and greater barons, severally by our letters; and we will moveover cause to be summoned generally, through our sheriffs and bailiffs, and others who hold of us in chief, for a fixed date, namely, after the expiry of at least forty days, and at a fixed place; and in all letters of such summons we will specify the reason of the summons. And when the summons has thus been made, the business shall proceed on the day appointed, according to the counsel of such as are present, although not all who were summoned have come.

15. We will not for the future grant to anyone license to take an aid from his own free tenants, except to ransom his person, to make his eldest son a knight, and once to marry his eldest daughter; and on each of these occasions there shall be levied only a reasonable aid.

16. No one shall be distrained for performance of greater service for a knight's fee, or for any other free tenement, than is due therefrom.

17. Common pleas shall not follow our court, but shall be held in some fixed place.

18. Inquests of novel disseisin, of mort d'ancestor, and of darrein presentment shall not be held elsewhere than in their own county courts, and that in manner following; We, or, if we should be out of the realm, our chief justiciar, will send two justiciaries through every county four times a year, who shall alone with four knights of the county chosen by the county, hold the said assizes in the county court, on the day and in the place of meeting of that court.

19. And if any of the said assizes cannot be taken on the day of the county court, let there remain of the knights and freeholders, who were present at the county court on that day, as many as may be required for the efficient making of judgments, according as the business be more or less.

20. A freeman shall not be amerced for a slight offense, except in accordance with the degree of the offense; and for a grave offense he shall be amerced in accordance with the gravity of the offense, yet saving always his "contentment"; and a merchant in the same way, saving his "merchandise"; and a villein shall be amerced in the same way, saving his "wainage" if they have fallen into our mercy: and none of the aforesaid amercements shall be imposed except by the oath of honest men of the neighborhood.

21. Earls and barons shall not be amerced except through their peers, and only in accordance with the degree of the offense.

22. A clerk shall not be amerced in respect of his lay holding except after the manner of the others aforesaid; further, he shall not be amerced in accordance with the extent of his ecclesiastical benefice.

23. No village or individual shall be compelled to make bridges at river banks, except those who from of old were legally bound to do so.

24. No sheriff, constable, coroners, or others of our bailiffs, shall hold pleas of our Crown.

25. All counties, hundred, wapentakes, and trithings (except our demesne manors) shall remain at the old rents, and without any additional payment.

26. If anyone holding of us a lay fief shall die, and our sheriff or bailiff shall exhibit our letters patent of summons for a debt which the deceased owed us, it shall be lawful for our sheriff or bailiff to attach and enroll the chattels of the deceased, found upon the lay fief, to the value of that debt, at the sight of law worthy men, provided always that nothing whatever be thence removed until the debt which is evident shall be fully paid to us; and the residue shall be left to the executors to fulfill the will of the deceased; and if there be nothing due from him to us, all the chattels shall go to the deceased, saving to his wife and children their reasonable shares.

27. If any freeman shall die intestate, his chattels shall be distributed by the hands of his nearest kinsfolk and friends, under supervision of the Church, saving to every one the debts which the deceased owed to him.

28. No constable or other bailiff of ours shall take corn or other provisions from anyone without immediately tendering money therefor, unless he can have postponement thereof by permission of the seller.

29. No constable shall compel any knight to give money in lieu of castle-guard, when he is willing to perform it in his own person, or (if he himself cannot do it from

any reasonable cause) then by another responsible man. Further, if we have led or sent him upon military service, he shall be relieved from guard in proportion to the time during which he has been on service because of us.

30. No sheriff or bailiff of ours, or other person, shall take the horses or carts of any freeman for transport duty, against the will of the said freeman.

31. Neither we nor our bailiffs shall take, for our castles or for any other work of ours, wood which is not ours, against the will of the owner of that wood.

32. We will not retain beyond one year and one day, the lands those who have been convicted of felony, and the lands shall thereafter be handed over to the lords of the fiefs.

33. All kydells for the future shall be removed altogether from Thames and Medway, and throughout all England, except upon the seashore.

34. The writ which is called praecipe shall not for the future be issued to anyone, regarding any tenement whereby a freeman may lose his court.

35. Let there be one measure of wine throughout our whole realm; and one measure of ale; and one measure of corn, to wit, "the London quarter"; and one width of cloth (whether dyed, or russet, or "halberget"), to wit, two ells within the selvedges; of weights also let it be as of measures.

36. Nothing in future shall be given or taken for a writ of inquisition of life or limbs, but freely it shall be granted, and never denied.

37. If anyone holds of us by fee-farm, either by socage

or by burage, or of any other land by knight's service, we will not (by reason of that fee-farm, socage, or burgage), have the wardship of the heir, or of such land of his as if of the fief of that other; nor shall we have wardship of that fee-farm, socage, or burgage, unless such fee-farm owes knight's service. We will not by reason of any small serjeancy which anyone may hold of us by the service of rendering to us knives, arrows, or the like, have wardship of his heir or of the land which he holds of another lord by knight's service.

38. No bailiff for the future shall, upon his own unsupported complaint, put anyone to his "law", without credible witnesses brought for this purposes.

39. No freemen shall be taken or imprisoned or disseised or exiled or in any way destroyed, nor will we go upon him nor send upon him, except by the lawful judgment of his peers or by the law of the land.

40. To no one will we sell, to no one will we refuse or delay, right or justice.

41. All merchants shall have safe and secure exit from England, and entry to England, with the right to tarry there and to move about as well by land as by water, for buying and selling by the ancient and right customs, quit from all evil tolls, except (in time of war) such merchants as are of the land at war with us. And if such are found in our land at the beginning of the war, they shall be detained, without injury to their bodies or goods, until information be received by us, or by our chief justiciar, how the merchants of our land found in the land at war with us are treated; and if our men are safe there, the others shall be safe in our land.

42. It shall be lawful in future for anyone (excepting

always those imprisoned or outlawed in accordance with the law of the kingdom, and natives of any country at war with us, and merchants, who shall be treated as if above provided) to leave our kingdom and to return, safe and secure by land and water, except for a short period in time of war, on grounds of public policy- reserving always the allegiance due to us.

43. If anyone holding of some escheat (such as the honor of Wallingford, Nottingham, Boulogne, Lancaster, or of other escheats which are in our hands and are baronies) shall die, his heir shall give no other relief, and perform no other service to us than he would have done to the baron if that barony had been in the baron's hand; and we shall hold it in the same manner in which the baron held it.

44. Men who dwell without the forest need not henceforth come before our justiciaries of the forest upon a general summons, unless they are in plea, or sureties of one or more, who are attached for the forest.

45. We will appoint as justices, constables, sheriffs, or bailiffs only such as know the law of the realm and mean to observe it well.

46. All barons who have founded abbeys, concerning which they hold charters from the kings of England, or of which they have long continued possession, shall have the wardship of them, when vacant, as they ought to have.

47. All forests that have been made such in our time shall forthwith be disafforsted; and a similar course shall be followed with regard to river banks that have been placed "in defense" by us in our time.

48. All evil customs connected with forests and warrens, foresters and warreners, sheriffs and their officers, river banks and their wardens, shall immediately by inquired into in each county by twelve sworn knights of the same county chosen by the honest men of the same county, and shall, within forty days of the said inquest, be utterly abolished, so as never to be restored, provided always that we previously have intimation thereof, or our justiciar, if we should not be in England.

49. We will immediately restore all hostages and charters delivered to us by Englishmen, as sureties of the peace of faithful service.

50. We will entirely remove from their bailiwicks, the relations of Gerard of Athee (so that in future they shall have no bailiwick in England); namely, Engelard of Cigogne, Peter, Guy, and Andrew of Chanceaux, Guy of Cigogne, Geoffrey of Martigny with his brothers, Philip Mark with his brothers and his nephew Geoffrey, and the whole brood of the same.

51. As soon as peace is restored, we will banish from the kingdom all foreign born knights, crossbowmen, serjeants, and mercenary soldiers who have come with horses and arms to the kingdom's hurt.

52. If anyone has been dispossessed or removed by us, without the legal judgment of his peers, from his lands, castles, franchises, or from his right, we will immediately restore them to him; and if a dispute arise over this, then let it be decided by the five and twenty barons of whom mention is made below in the clause for securing the peace. Moreover, for all those possessions, from which anyone has, without the lawful judgment of his peers, been disseised or removed, by our father, King Henry,

or by our brother, King Richard, and which we retain in our hand (or which as possessed by others, to whom we are bound to warrant them) we shall have respite until the usual term of crusaders; excepting those things about which a plea has been raised, or an inquest made by our order, before our taking of the cross; but as soon as we return from the expedition, we will immediately grant full justice therein.

53. We shall have, moreover, the same respite and in the same manner in rendering justice concerning the disafforestation or retention of those forests which Henry our father and Richard our brother afforested, and concerning the wardship of lands which are of the fief of another (namely, such wardships as we have hitherto had by reason of a fief which anyone held of us by knight's service), and concerning abbeys founded on other fiefs than our own, in which the lord of the fee claims to have right; and when we have returned, or if we desist from our expedition, we will immediately grant full justice to all who complain of such things.

54. No one shall be arrested or imprisoned upon the appeal of a woman, for the death of any other than her husband.

55. All fines made with us unjustly and against the law of the land, and all amercements, imposed unjustly and against the law of the land, shall be entirely remitted, or else it shall be done concerning them according to the decision of the five and twenty barons whom mention is made below in the clause for securing the pease, or according to the judgment of the majority of the same, along with the aforesaid Stephen, archbishop of Canterbury, if he can be present, and such others as he may wish to bring with him for this purpose, and

if he cannot be present the business shall nevertheless proceed without him, provided always that if any one or more of the aforesaid five and twenty barons are in a similar suit, they shall be removed as far as concerns this particular judgment, others being substituted in their places after having been selected by the rest of the same five and twenty for this purpose only, and after having been sworn.

56. If we have disseised or removed Welshmen from lands or liberties, or other things, without the legal judgment of their peers in England or in Wales, they shall be immediately restored to them; and if a dispute arise over this, then let it be decided in the marches by the judgment of their peers; for the tenements in England according to the law of England, for tenements in Wales according to the law of Wales, and for tenements in the marches according to the law of the marches. Welshmen shall do the same to us and ours.

57. Further, for all those possessions from which any Welshman has, without the lawful judgment of his peers, been disseised or removed by King Henry our father, or King Richard our brother, and which we retain in our hand (or which are possessed by others, and which we ought to warrant), we will have respite until the usual term of crusaders; excepting those things about which a plea has been raised or an inquest made by our order before we took the cross; but as soon as we return (or if perchance we desist from our expedition), we will immediately grant full justice in accordance with the laws of the Welsh and in relation to the foresaid regions.

58. We will immediately give up the son of Llywelyn and all the hostages of Wales, and the charters delivered to us as security for the peace.

59. We will do towards Alexander, king of Scots, concerning the return of his sisters and his hostages, and concerning his franchises, and his right, in the same manner as we shall do towards our other barons of England, unless it ought to be otherwise according to the charters which we hold from William his father, formerly king of Scots; and this shall be according to the judgment of his peers in our court.

60. Moreover, all these aforesaid customs and liberties, the observances of which we have granted in our kingdom as far as pertains to us towards our men, shall be observed b all of our kingdom, as well clergy as laymen, as far as pertains to them towards their men.

61. Since, moveover, for God and the amendment of our kingdom and for the better allaying of the quarrel that has arisen between us and our barons, we have granted all these concessions, desirous that they should enjoy them in complete and firm endurance forever, we give and grant to them the underwritten security, namely, that the barons choose five and twenty barons of the kingdom, whomsoever they will, who shall be bound with all their might, to observe and hold, and cause to be observed, the peace and liberties we have granted and confirmed to them by this our present Charter, so that if we, or our justiciar, or our bailiffs or any one of our officers, shall in anything be at fault towards anyone, or shall have broken any one of the articles of this peace or of this security, and the offense be notified to four barons of the foresaid five and twenty, the said four barons shall repair to us (or our justiciar, if we are out of the realm) and, laying the transgression before us, petition to have that transgression redressed without delay. And if we shall not have corrected the transgression (or, in the event of

our being out of the realm, if our justiciar shall not have corrected it) within forty days, reckoning from the time it has been intimated to us (or to our justiciar, if we should be out of the realm), the four barons aforesaid shall refer that matter to the rest of the five and twenty barons, and those five and twenty barons shall, together with the community of the whole realm, distrain and distress us in all possible ways, namely, by seizing our castles, lands, possessions, and in any other way they can, until redress has been obtained as they deem fit, saving harmless our own person, and the persons of our queen and children; and when redress has been obtained, they shall resume their old relations towards us. And let whoever in the country desires it, swear to obey the orders of the said five and twenty barons for the execution of all the aforesaid matters, and along with them, to molest us to the utmost of his power; and we publicly and freely grant leave to everyone who wishes to swear, and we shall never forbid anyone to swear.

All those, moveover, in the land who of themselves and of their own accord are unwilling to swear to the twenty five to help them in constraining and molesting us, we shall by our command compel the same to swear to the effect foresaid. And if any one of the five and twenty barons shall have died or departed from the land, or be incapacitated in any other manner which would prevent the foresaid provisions being carried out, those of the said twenty five barons who are left shall choose another in his place according to their own judgment, and he shall be sworn in the same way as the others. Further, in all matters, the execution of which is entrusted to these twenty five barons, if perchance these twenty five are present and disagree about anything, or if some of them, after being summoned, are unwilling or unable to be present, that which the majority of those present ordain or command shall be held as fixed and established, exactly as if the whole twenty five had concurred in this; and the said twenty five shall swear that they will faithfully observe all that is aforesaid, and cause it to be observed with all their might. And we shall procure nothing from anyone, directly or indirectly, whereby any part of these concessions and liberties might be revoked or diminished; and if any such things has been procured, let it be void and null, and we shall never use it personally or by another.

62. And all the will, hatreds, and bitterness that have arisen between us and our men, clergy and lay, from the date of the quarrel, we have completely remitted and pardoned to everyone. Moreover, all trespasses occasioned by the said quarrel, from Easter in the sixteenth year of our reign till the restoration of peace, we have fully remitted to all, both clergy and laymen, and completely forgiven, as far as pertains to us. And on this head, we have caused to be made for them letters testimonial patent of the lord Stephen, archbishop of Canterbury, of the lord Henry, archbishop of Dublin, of the bishops aforesaid, and of Master Pandulf as touching this security and the concessions aforesaid.

63. Wherefore we will and firmly order that the English Church be free, and that the men in our kingdom have and hold all the aforesaid liberties, rights, and concessions, well and peaceably, freely and quietly, fully and wholly, for themselves and their heirs, of us and our heirs, in all respects and in all places forever, as is aforesaid. An oath, moreover, has been taken, as well on our part as on the part of the barons, that all these conditions aforesaid shall be kept in good faith and without evil intent. Given

under our hand - the above named and many others being witnesses - in the meadow which is called Runnymede, between Windsor and Staines, on the fifteenth day of June, in the seventeenth year of our reign.

ENGLISH BILL *of* RIGHTS, 1689

An Act Declaring the Rights and Liberties of the Subject and Settling the Succession of the Crown

Whereas the Lords Spiritual and Temporal and Commons assembled at Westminster, lawfully, fully and freely representing all the estates of the people of this realm, did upon the thirteenth day of February in the year of our Lord one thousand six hundred eighty-eight [old style date] present unto their Majesties, then called and known by the names and style of William and Mary, prince and princess of Orange, being present in their proper persons, a certain declaration in writing made by the said Lords and Commons in the words following, viz.:

Whereas the late King James the Second, by the assistance of divers evil counsellors, judges and ministers employed by him, did endeavour to subvert and extirpate the Protestant religion and the laws and liberties of this kingdom;

By assuming and exercising a power of dispensing with and suspending of laws and the execution of laws without consent of Parliament;

By committing and prosecuting divers worthy prelates for humbly petitioning to be excused from concurring to the said assumed power;

By issuing and causing to be executed a commission under the great seal for erecting a court called the Court of Commissioners for Ecclesiastical Causes;

By levying money for and to the use of the Crown by pretence of prerogative for other time and in other manner than the same was granted by Parliament;

By raising and keeping a standing army within this kingdom in time of peace without consent of Parliament, and quartering soldiers contrary to law;

By causing several good subjects being Protestants to be disarmed at the same time when papists were both armed and employed contrary to law;

By violating the freedom of election of members to serve in Parliament;

By prosecutions in the Court of King's Bench for matters and causes cognizable only in Parliament, and by divers other arbitrary and illegal courses;

And whereas of late years partial corrupt and unqualified persons have been returned and served on juries in trials, and particularly divers jurors in trials for high treason which were not freeholders;

And excessive bail hath been required of persons committed in criminal cases to elude the benefit of the laws made for the liberty of the subjects;

And excessive fines have been imposed;

And illegal and cruel punishments inflicted;

And several grants and promises made of fines and forfeitures before any conviction or judgment against the persons upon whom the same were to be levied;

All which are utterly and directly contrary to the known laws and statutes and freedom of this realm;

And whereas the said late King James the Second having abdicated the government and the throne being thereby vacant, his Highness the prince of Orange (whom it hath pleased Almighty God to make the glorious instrument of delivering this kingdom from popery and arbitrary power) did (by the advice of the Lords Spiritual and Temporal and divers principal persons of the Commons) cause letters to be written to the Lords Spiritual and Temporal being Protestants, and other letters to the several counties, cities, universities, boroughs and cinque ports, for the choosing of such persons to represent them as were of right to be sent to Parliament, to meet and sit at Westminster upon the two and twentieth day of January in this year one thousand six hundred eighty and eight [old style date], in order to such an establishment as that their religion, laws and liberties might not again be in danger of being subverted, upon which letters elections having been accordingly made;

And thereupon the said Lords Spiritual and Temporal and Commons, pursuant to their respective letters and elections, being now assembled in a full and free representative of this nation, taking into their most serious consideration the best means for attaining the ends aforesaid, do in the first place (as their ancestors in like case have usually done) for the vindicating and asserting their ancient rights and liberties declare

That the pretended power of suspending the laws or the execution of laws by regal authority without consent of Parliament is illegal;

That the pretended power of dispensing with laws or the execution of laws by regal authority, as it hath been assumed and exercised of late, is illegal;

That the commission for erecting the late Court of Commissioners for Ecclesiastical Causes, and all other commissions and courts of like nature, are illegal and pernicious;

That levying money for or to the use of the Crown by pretence of prerogative, without grant of Parliament, for longer time, or in other manner than the same is or shall be granted, is illegal;

That it is the right of the subjects to petition the king, and all commitments and prosecutions for such petitioning are illegal;

That the raising or keeping a standing army within the kingdom in time of peace, unless it be with consent of Parliament, is against law;

That the subjects which are Protestants may have arms for their defence suitable to their conditions and as allowed by law;

That election of members of Parliament ought to be free;

That the freedom of speech and debates or proceedings in Parliament ought not to be impeached or questioned in any court or place out of Parliament;

That excessive bail ought not to be required, nor excessive fines imposed, nor cruel and unusual punishments inflicted;

That jurors ought to be duly impanelled and returned, and jurors which pass upon men in trials for high treason ought to be freeholders;

That all grants and promises of fines and forfeitures of particular persons before conviction are illegal and void;

And that for redress of all grievances, and for the amending, strengthening and preserving of the laws, Parliaments ought to be held frequently.

And they do claim, demand and insist upon all and singular the premises as their undoubted rights and liberties, and that no declarations, judgments, doings or proceedings to the prejudice of the people in any of the said premises ought in any wise to be drawn hereafter into consequence or example; to which demand of their rights they are particularly encouraged by the declaration of his Highness the prince of Orange as being the only means for obtaining a full redress and remedy therein. Having therefore an entire confidence that his said Highness the prince of Orange will perfect the deliverance so far advanced by him, and will still preserve them from the violation of their rights which they have here asserted, and from all other attempts upon their religion, rights and liberties, the said Lords Spiritual and Temporal and Commons assembled at Westminster do resolve that William and Mary, prince and princess of Orange, be and be declared king and queen of England, France and Ireland and the dominions thereunto belonging, to hold the crown and royal dignity of the said kingdoms and dominions to them, the said prince and princess, during their lives and the life of the survivor to them, and that the sole and full exercise of the regal power be only in and executed by the said prince of Orange in the names of the said prince and princess during their joint lives, and after their deceases the said crown and royal dignity of the same kingdoms and dominions to be to the heirs of the body of the said princess, and for default of such issue to the Princess Anne of Denmark and the heirs of her body, and for default of such issue to the heirs of the body of the said prince of Orange. And the Lords

Spiritual and Temporal and Commons do pray the said prince and princess to accept the same accordingly.

And that the oaths hereafter mentioned be taken by all persons of whom the oaths have allegiance and supremacy might be required by law, instead of them; and that the said oaths of allegiance and supremacy be abrogated.

I, A.B., do sincerely promise and swear that I will be faithful and bear true allegiance to their Majesties King William and Queen Mary. So help me God.

I, A.B., do swear that I do from my heart abhor, detest and abjure as impious and heretical this damnable doctrine and position, that princes excommunicated or deprived by the Pope or any authority of the see of Rome may be deposed or murdered by their subjects or any other whatsoever. And I do declare that no foreign prince, person, prelate, state or potentate hath or ought to have any jurisdiction, power, superiority, pre-eminence or authority, ecclesiastical or spiritual, within this realm. So help me God.

Upon which their said Majesties did accept the crown and royal dignity of the kingdoms of England, France and Ireland, and the dominions thereunto belonging, according to the resolution and desire of the said Lords and Commons contained in the said declaration. And thereupon their Majesties were pleased that the said Lords Spiritual and Temporal and Commons, being the two Houses of Parliament, should continue to sit, and with their Majesties' royal concurrence make effectual provision for the settlement of the religion, laws and liberties of this kingdom, so that the same for the future might not be in danger again of being subverted, to which the said Lords Spiritual and Temporal and Commons did agree, and proceed to act accordingly. Now in pursuance of the premises the said Lords Spiritual and Temporal and Commons in Parliament assembled, for the ratifying, confirming and establishing the said declaration and the articles, clauses, matters and things therein contained by the force of law made in due form by authority of Parliament, do pray that it may be declared and enacted that all and singular the rights and liberties asserted and claimed in the said declaration are the true, ancient and indubitable rights and liberties of the people of this kingdom, and so shall be esteemed, allowed, adjudged, deemed and taken to be; and that all and every the particulars aforesaid shall be firmly and strictly holden and observed as they are expressed in the said declaration, and all officers and ministers whatsoever shall serve their Majesties and their successors according to the same in all time to come. And the said Lords Spiritual and Temporal and Commons, seriously considering how it hath pleased Almighty God in his marvellous providence and merciful goodness to this nation to provide and preserve their said Majesties' royal persons most happily to reign over us upon the throne of their ancestors, for which they render unto him from the bottom of their hearts their humblest thanks and praises, do truly, firmly, assuredly and in the sincerity of their hearts think, and do hereby recognize, acknowledge and declare, that King James the Second having abdicated the government, and their Majesties having accepted the crown and royal dignity as aforesaid, their said Majesties did become, were, are and of right ought to be by the laws of this realm our sovereign liege lord and lady, king and queen of England, France and Ireland and the dominions thereunto belonging, in and to whose princely persons the royal state, crown and dignity of the said realms with all honours, styles, titles, regalities, prerogatives, powers, jurisdictions and authorities to the same belonging and appertaining are most fully, rightfully and entirely invested and incorporated, united and annexed. And for preventing all questions and divisions in this realm by reason of any pretended titles to the crown, and for preserving a certainty in the succession thereof, in and upon which the unity, peace, tranquility and safety of this nation doth under God wholly consist and depend, the said Lords Spiritual and Temporal and Commons do beseech their Majesties that it may be enacted, established and declared, that the crown and regal government of the said kingdoms and dominions, with all and singular the premises thereunto belonging and appertaining, shall be and continue to their said Majesties and the survivor of them during their lives and the life of the survivor of them, and that the entire, perfect and full exercise of the regal power and government be only in and executed by his Majesty in the names of both their Majesties during their joint lives; and after their deceases the said crown and premises shall be and remain to the heirs of the body of her Majesty, and for default of such issue to her Royal Highness the Princess Anne of Denmark and the heirs of the body of his said Majesty; and thereunto the said Lords Spiritual and Temporal and Commons do in the name of all the people aforesaid most humbly and faithfully submit themselves, their heirs and posterities for ever, and do faithfully promise that they will stand to, maintain and defend their said Majesties, and also the limitation and succession of the crown herein specified and contained, to the utmost of their powers with their lives and estates against all persons whatsoever that shall attempt anything to the contrary. And whereas it hath been found by experience that it is inconsistent with the safety and welfare of this Protestant kingdom to be governed by a popish prince, or by any king or queen marrying a papist, the said Lords Spiritual and Temporal and Commons do further pray that it may be enacted, that all and every person and persons that is, are or shall be reconciled to or shall hold communion with the see or Church of Rome, or shall profess the popish religion, or shall marry a papist, shall be excluded and be for ever incapable to inherit, possess or enjoy the crown and government of this realm and Ireland and the dominions thereunto belonging or any part of the same, or to have, use or exercise any regal power, authority or jurisdiction within the same; and in all and every such case or cases the people of these realms shall be and are hereby absolved of their allegiance; and the said crown and government shall from time to time descend to and be enjoyed by such person or persons being Protestants as should have inherited and enjoyed the same in case the said person or persons so reconciled, holding communion or professing or marrying as aforesaid were naturally dead; and that every king and queen of this realm who at any time hereafter shall come to and succeed in the imperial crown of this kingdom shall on the first day of the meeting of the first Parliament next after his or her coming to the crown, sitting in his or her throne in the House of Peers in the presence of the Lords and Commons therein assembled, or at his or her coronation before such person or persons who shall administer the coronation oath to him or her at the time of his or her taking the said oath (which shall first happen), make, subscribe and audibly repeat the declaration mentioned in the statute made in the thirtieth year of the reign of King Charles the Second entitled, _An Act for the more effectual preserving the king's person and government by disabling papists from sitting in either House of Parliament._ But if it shall happen that such king or queen upon his or her succession to the crown of this realm shall be under the age of twelve years, then every such king or queen shall make, subscribe and audibly repeat the same declaration at his or her coronation or the first day of the meeting of the first Parliament as aforesaid which shall first happen after such king or queen shall have attained the said age of twelve years. All which their Majesties are contented and pleased shall be declared, enacted and established by authority of this present Parliament, and shall stand, remain and be the law of this realm for ever; and the same are by their said Majesties, by and with the advice and consent of the Lords Spiritual and Temporal and Commons in Parliament assembled and by the authority of the same, declared, enacted and established accordingly.

II. And be it further declared and enacted by the authority aforesaid, that from and after this present session of Parliament no dispensation by _non obstante_ of or to any statute or any part thereof shall be allowed, but that the same shall be held void and of no effect, except a dispensation be allowed of in such statute, and except in such cases as shall be specially provided for by one or more bill or bills to be passed during this present session of Parliament.

III. Provided that no charter or grant or pardon granted before the three and twentieth day of October in the year of our Lord one thousand six hundred eighty-nine shall be any ways impeached or invalidated by this Act, but that the same shall be and remain of the same force and effect in law and no other than as if this Act had never been made.

ACT *of* UNION, 1707

Act ratifying and approving treaty of the two Kingdoms of Scotland and England.

The Estates of Parliament, considering that Articles of Union of the Kingdoms of Scotland and England were agreed on 22nd of July, 1706 by the Commissioners nominated on behalf of this Kingdom, under Her Majesties Great Seal of Scotland bearing date the 27th of February last past, in pursuance of the fourth Act of the third Session of this Parliament and the Commissioners nominated on behalf of the Kingdom of England under Her Majesties Great Seal of England bearing date at Westminster the tenth day of April last past in pursuance of an Act of Parliament made in England the third year of Her Majesties Reign to treat of and concerning an Union of the said Kingdoms Which Articles were in all humility presented to Her Majesty upon the twenty third of the said Month of July and were Recommended to this Parliament by Her Majesties Royal Letter of the date the 31st day of July, 1706; and that the said Estates of Parliament have agreed to, and approve of the said Articles of Union, with some additions.

And that the said Estates of Parliament have agreed to and approve of the said Articles of Union with some Additions and Explanations as is contained in the Articles hereafter insert And sicklyke Her Majesty with advice and consent of the Estates of Parliament Resolving to Establish the Protestant Religion and Presbyterian Church Government within this Kingdom has past in this Session of Parliament an Act entituled Act for secureing of the Protestant Religion and Presbyterian Church Government which by the Tenor thereof is appointed to be insert in any Act ratifying the Treaty and expressly declared to be a fundamentall and essentiall Condition of the said Treaty or Union in all time coming.

Therefore Her Majesty with advice and consent of the Estates of Parliament in fortification of the Approbation of the Articles as above mentioned And for their further and better Establishment of the same upon full and mature deliberation upon the forsaids Articles of Union and Act of Parliament Doth Ratifie Approve and Confirm the same with the Additions and Explanations contained in the saids Articles in manner and under the provision aftermentioned whereof the Tenor follows.

Article 1: That the Two Kingdoms of Scotland and England, shall upon the 1st May next ensuing the date hereof, and forever after, be United into One Kingdom by the Name of GREAT BRITAIN: And that the Ensigns Armorial of the said United Kingdom be such as Her Majesty shall think fit, and used in all Flags, Banners, Standards and Ensigns both at Sea and Land.

Article 2: That the Succession to the Monarchy of the United Kingdom of Great Britain and of the Dominions thereunto belonging after Her Most Sacred Majesty, and in default of Issue of Her Majesty be, remain and continue to the Most Excellent Princess Sophia Electoress and Dutchess Dowager of Hanover, and the Heirs of Her body, being Protestants, upon whom the Crown of England is settled by an Act of Parliament made in England in the twelth year of the Reign of His late Majesty King William the Third entituled An Act for the further Limitation of the Crown and better securing the Rights and Liberties of the Subject;

And that all Papists and persons marrying Papists, shall be excluded from and forever incapable to inherit possess or enjoy the Imperial Crown of Great Britain, and the Dominions thereunto belonging or any part thereof; And in every such case the Crown and Government shall from time to time descend to, and be enjoyed by such person being a Protestant as should have inherited and enjoyed the same, in case such Papists or person marrying a Papist was naturally dead, according to the provision for the Descent of the Crown of England, made by another Act of Parliament in England in the first year of the Reign of their late Majesties King William and Queen Mary entituled an Act declaring the Rights and Liberties of the Subject, and settling the Succession of the Crown.

Article 3: That the United Kingdom of Great Britain be Represented by one and the same Parliament, to be stiled the Parliament of Great Britain.

Article 4: That the Subjects of the United Kingdom of Great Britain shall from and after the Union have full Freedom and Intercourse of Trade and Navigation to and from any port or place within the said United Kingdom and the Dominions and Plantations thereunto belonging. And that there be a Communication of all other Rights, Privileges and Advantages which do or may belong to the Subjects of either Kingdom except where it is otherwayes expressly agreed in these Articles.

Article 5: That all ships or vessels belonging to Her Majesties Subjects of Scotland at the time of Ratifying the Treaty of Union of the Two Kingdoms in the Parliament of Scotland though foreign built be deemed and pass as ships of the build of Great Britain; the Owner or where there are more Owners, one or more of the Owners within Twelve Months after the first of May next making oath that at the time of Ratifying the Treaty of Union in the Parliament of Scotland, the same did in haill or in part belong to him or them, or to some other Subject of Subjects of Scotland, to be particularly named with the place of their respective abodes, and that the same doth then at the time of the said Deposition wholly belong to him or them, and that no forreigner directly or indirectly hath any share part or interest therein, Which Oath shall be made before the chief Officer or Officers of the Customs in the Port next to the abode of the said Owner or Owners;

And the said Officer or Officers shall be Impowered to administer the said Oath, And the Oath being so administred shall be attested by the Officer or Officers who administred the same And being Registred by the said Officer or Officers, shall be delivered to the Master of the ship for security of her Navigation and a Duplicate thereof shall be transmitted by the said Officer or Officers to the Chief Officer or Officers of the Customs in the port of Edinburgh, to be there Entered in a Register and from thence to be sent to the port of London to be there Entered in the General Register of all Trading ships belonging to Great Britain.

Article 6: That all parts of the United Kingdom for ever from and after the Union shall have the same Allowances, Encouragements and Drawbacks, and be under the same Prohibitions, Restrictions and Regulations of Trade and lyable to the same Customs and Duties on Import and Export. And that the Allowances Encouragements and Drawbacks Prohibitions Restrictions and Regulations of Trade and the Customs and Duties on Import and Export settled in England when the Union commences shall from and after the Union take place throughout the whole

United Kingdom, excepting and reserving the Duties upon Export and Import of such particular Commodities from which any persons the Subjects of either Kingdom are specially Liberated and Exempted by their private Rights which after the Union are to remain safe and entire to them in all respects as before the same.

And that from and after the Union no Scots Cattle carried into England shall be lyable to any other Duties either on the publick or private Accounts than these Duties to which the Cattle of England are or shall be lyable within the said Kindgom. And seeing by the Laws of England there are Rewards granted upon the Exportation of certain kinds of Grain wherein Oats grinded or ungrinded are not expressed, that from and after the Union when Oats shall be sold at 15 shillings Sterling per quarter of the Oat-meal exported in the terms of the Law whereby and so long as Rewards are granted for Exportation of other Grains. And that the Bear of Scotland have the same Rewards as Barley.

And in respect the Importation of Victual into Scotland from any place beyond Sea would prove a Discouragement to Tillage, Therefore that the Prohibition as now in force by the Law of Scotland against Importation of Victual from Ireland or any other place beyond Sea into Scotland, do after the Union remain in the same force as now it is until more proper and effectuall ways be provided by the Parliament of Great Britain for discouraging the Importation of the said Victual from beyond Sea.

Article 7: That all parts of the United Kingdom be for ever from and after the Union lyable to the same Excises upon all Exciseable Liquors excepting only that the 34 Gallons English Barrel of Beer or Ale amounting to 12 Gallons Scots present measure sold in Scotland by the

Brewer at 9/6d Sterling excluding all Duties and Retailed including Duties and the Retailer's profit at 2d the Scots pint or eight part of the Scots Gallon, be not after the Union lyable on account of the present Excise upon Exciseable Liquors in England, to any higher Imposition than 2s Sterling upon the forsaid 34 Gallons English barrel, being 12 gallons the present Scots measure And that the Excise settled in England on all other Liquors when the Union commences take place throughout the whole United Kingdom.

Article 8: That from and after the Union all forreign Salt which shall be Imported into Scotland shall be charged at the Importation there with the same Duties as the like Salt is now charged with being Imported into England and to be levied and secured in the same manner. But in regard the Duties of great quantities of forreign Salt Imported may be very heavie on the Merchants Importers; That therefor all forreign Salt imported into Scotland shall be Cellared and Locked up under the custody of the Merchant Importer and the Officers imployed for levying the Duties upon Salt And that the Merchant may have what quantities thereof his occasion may require not under a Weigh or fourtie Bushells at a time; Giving security for the duty of what quantity he receives payable in six Months. But Scotland shall for the space of seven Years from the said Union be Exempted from paying in Scotland for Salt made there the Dutie or Excise now payable for Salt made in England:

But from the Expiration of the said seven years shall be subject and lyable to the same Duties for Salt make in Scotland, as shall be then payable for Salt made in England, to be levied and secured in the same manner and with proportional Drawbacks and Allowances as in

England, with this exception that Scotland shall after the said seven years remain exempted from the Duty of 2s 4d a Bushell on home Salt Imposed by ane Act made in England in the Ninth and Tenth of King William the Third of England.

And if the Parliament of Great Britain shall at or before the expiring of the said seven years substitute any other fund in place of the said 2s 4d of Excise on the bushel of Home Salt, Scotland shall after the said seven years, bear a proportion of the said Fund, and have an Equivalent in the Terms of this Treaty, And that during the said seven years there shall be payed in England for all Salt made in Scotland and imported from thence into England the same duties upon the Importation as shall be payable for Salt made in England and levied and secured in the same manner as the Duties on forreign Salt are to be levied and secured in England.

And that after the said seven years how long the said Duty of 2s 4d a Bushel upon Salt is continued in England the said 2s 4d a Bushel shall be payable for all Salt made in Scotland and imported into England, to be levied and secured in the same manner And that during the continuance of the Duty of 2s 4d a Bushel upon Salt made in England no Salt whatsoever be brought from Scotland to England by Land in any manner under the penalty of forfeiting the Salt and the Cattle and Carriages made use of in bringing the same and paying 20s for every Bushel of such Salt, and proportionably for a greater or lesser quantity, for which the Carrier as well as the Owner shall be lyable jointly and severally, And the persons bringing or carrying the same, to be imprisoned by any one Justice of the Peace, by the space of six months without Bail, and until the penalty by payed:

And for Establishing an equality Trade That all Fleshes exported from Scotland to England and put on Board in Scotland to be Exported to parts beyond the Seas and provisions for ships in Scotland and for forreign voyages may be salted with Scots Salt paying the same Dutie for what Salt is so employed as the like quantity of such Salt pays in England and under the same penalties forfeitures and provisions for preventing of frauds as are mentioned in the Laws of England And that from and after the Union the Laws and Acts of Parliament in Scotland for Pineing Curing and Packing of Herrings White Fish and Salmond for Exportation with Forreign Salt only without any mixture of British or Irish Salt and for preventing of frauds in Curing and Packing of Fish be continued in force in Scotland subject to such alterations as shall be made by the Parliament of Great Britain.

And that all Fish exported from Scotland to parts beyond the Seas which shall be Cured with Forreign Salt only and without mixture of British or Irish Salt, shall have the same Eases Premiums and Drawbacks as are or shall be allowed to such persons as Export the like Fish from England: And that for Encouragement of the Herring Fishing there shall be allowed and payed to the Subjects Inhabitants of Great Britain during the present allowances for other Fishes 10s 5d Sterling for every Barrel of White Herrings which shall be exported from Scotland; And that there shall be allowed 5s Sterling for every Barrel of Beef of Pork salted with Forreign Salt without mixture of British or Irish Salt and Exported for sale from Scotland to parts beyond Sea alterable by the Parliament of Great Britain.

And if any matters of fraud relating to the said Duties on Salt shall hereafter appear which are not sufficiently provided against by this Article the same shall be subject to such further provisions as shall be thought fit by the Parliament of Great Britain.

Article 9: That whenever the sum of £1,997,763 8s 4d (and one) half penny shall be Enacted by the Parliament of Great Britain to be raised in that part of the United Kingdom now called England, on Land and other things usually charged in Acts of Parliament there for granting an aid to the Crown by a Land Tax; that part of the United Kingdom now called Scotland shall be charged by the same Act with a further sum of £48,000 free of all Charges, as the Quota of Scotland to such Tax, and so proportionably for any greater or lesser sum raised in England by any Tax on Land and other things usually charged, together with the Land And that such Quota for Scotland in the cases aforesaid, be raised and collected in the same manner as the Cess now is in Scotland, but subject to such Regulations in the manner of Collecting, as shall be made by the Parliament of Great Britain.

Article 10: That during the continuance of the respective Duties on Stampt paper, Vellom and Parchment, by the severall Acts now in force in England, Scotland shall not be charged with the same respective Duties.

Article 11: That during the continuance of the Duties payable in England on Windows and Lights which determines on 1st August 1710 Scotland shall not be charged with the same Duties.

Article 12: That during the continuance of the Duties payable in England on Coals, Culm and Cinders, which determines 30th September 1710 Scotland shall not be charged therewith for Coals Culm and Cinders consumed there but shall be charged with the same Duties as in

England for all Coals, Culm and Cinders not consumed in Scotland.

Article 13: That during the continuance of the Duty payable in England on Malt, which determines 24th June 1707, Scotland shall not be charged with that Duty.

Article 14: That the Kingdom of Scotland be not Charged with any other Duties laid on by the Parliament of England before the Union except these consented to in this Treaty, in regard it is agreed, That all necessary Provision shall be made by the Parliament of Scotland for the publick Charge and Service of that Kingdom for the year 1707: Provided nevertheless That if the Parliament of England shall think fit to lay any further Impositions by way of Customs, or such Excises, with which by virtue of this Treaty, Scotland is to be charged equally with England, in such case Scotland shall be lyable to the same Customs and Excises, and have an Equivalent to be settled by the Parliament of Great Britain;

With this further provision That any Malt to be made and consumed in that part of the United Kingdom now called Scotland shall not be charged with any Imposition upon Malt during this present War;

And seeing that it cannot be supposed that the Parliament of Great Britain will ever lay any sorts of Burthens upon the United Kingdom, but what they shall find necessity at that time for the Preservation and Good of the whole, and with due regard to the Circumstances and Abilities of every part of the United Kingdom Therefore it is agreed That there be no further Exemption insisted upon for any part of the United Kingdom, but that the consideration of any Exemption beyond that already agreed on in this Treaty, shall be left to the determination of the Parliament of Great Britain.

Article 15: Whereas by the Terms of this Treaty the Subjects of Scotland for preserving an Equality of Trade throughout the United Kingdom, will be lyable to severall Customs and Excises now payable in England, which will be applicable towards payment of the Debts of England, contracted before the Union;

It is agreed, That Scotland shall have an Equivalent for what the Subjects thereof shall be so charged towards payment of the said Debts of England, in all particulars whatsoever, in manner following viz.

That before the Union of the said Kingdoms, the sum of £398,085 10s be granted to Her Majesty by the Parliament of England for the uses aftermentioned, being the Equivalent to be answered to Scotland for such parts of the saids Customs and Excises upon all Exciseable Liquors, with which that Kingdom is to be charged upon the Union, as will be applicable to the payment of the said Debts of England, according to the proportions which the present Customs in Scotland, being £30,000 per annum : And which the present Excises on Excisable Liquors in Scotland, do bear to the Customs in England, computed at &pounds;1,341,559 per annum;

And which the present Excises on Excisable Liquors in Scotland, being £33,500 per annum, do bear to the Excises and Excisable Liquors in England, computed at £947,602 per annum; Which sum of £398,085 10s, shall be due and payable from the time of the Union:

And in regard That after the Union Scotland becoming lyable to the same Customs and Duties payable on Import and Export, and to the same Excises on all Exciseable Liquors as in England as well as upon that account as upon the account of the Increase of Trade and People

(which will be the happy consequence of the Union)*
the said Revenues will much improve beyond the before
mentioned annual values thereof, of which no present
Estimate can be made, Yet nevertheless for the reasons
aforesaid there ought to be a proportionable Equivalent
answered to Scotland It is agreed That after the Union
there shall be an Accompt kept of the said Duties arising
in Scotland, to the end it may appear, what ought to
be answered to Scotland, as an Equivalent for such
proportion of the said encrease as shall be applicable to
the payment of Debts of England.

And for the further and more effectuall answering the
severall ends hereafter mentioned It is agreed that from
and after the Union, the whole Encrease of the Revenues
of Customs, and Duties on Import and Export, and Excise
upon Exciseable Liquors in Scotland over and above the
annual produce of the said respective Duties, as above
stated, shall go and be applied, for the term of seven
years, to the uses hereafter mentioned; And that upon
the said account, there shall be answered to Scotland
annually from the end of seven years after the Union, an
Equivalent in proportion to such part of the said Increase
as shall be applicable to the Debts of England, And
generally that an Equivalent shall be answered to;

And as for the uses to which the said sum of £398,085
10s to be granted as aforesaid and all other monies,
which are to be answered or allowed to Scotland as said
is are to be applied It is agreed That in the first place out
of the foresaid sum what consideration shall be found
necessary to be had for any Losses which privat persons
may sustain by reducing the Coin of Scotland to the
Standard and Value of the Coin of England may be made
good In the next place That the Capital Stock or fund of

the African and Indian Company of Scotland advanced together with the interest for the said Capital Stock after the rate of 5% per annum from the respective times of the payment thereof shall be payed; Upon payment of which Capital Stock and Interest It is agreed The said Company be dissolved and cease And also that from the time of passing the Act of Parliament in England for raising the said sum of £398,085 10s the said Company shall neither Trade nor Grant Licence to Trade Providing that if the said Stock and Interest shall not be payed in twelve months after the Commencement of the Union That then the said Company may from thence forward Trade or give Licence to Trade until the said hail Capital Stock and Interest shall be payed:

And as to the Overplus of the said sum of £398,085 10s after payment of what consideration shall be had for losses in repairing the Coin and paying the said Capital Stock and Interest, and also the hail increase of the said Revenues of Customs Duties and Excises above the present value which shall arise in Scotland during the said term of seven years together with the Equivalent which shall become due upon the Improvement thereof in Scotland after the said term and also as to all other sums which according to the agreements aforesaid may become payable to Scotland by way of Equivalent for what that Kingdom shall hereafter become Scotland for such parts of the English Debts as Scotland may hereafter become lyable to pay by reason of the Union, other than such for which appropriations have been made by Parliament in England of the Customs, or other duties on Export and Import Excises on all Exciseable Liquors, in respect of which Debts, Equivalents are herein before provided.

Article 16: That from and after the Union the Coin shall be of the same standard and value, throughout the United Kingdom, as now in England, And a Mint shall be continued in Scotland under the same Rules as the Mint in England And the present Officers of the Mint continued subject to such Regulations and Alterations as Her Majesty Her Heirs or Successors, or the Parliament of Great Britain shall think fit.

Article 17: That from and after the Union the same Weights and Measures shall be used throughout the United Kingdom as are now Established in England; And Standards of Weights and Measures shall be kept by those Burroughs in Scotland, to whom the keeping the Standards of Weights and Measures now in use there does of speciall Right belong; All which Standards shall be sent down to such respective Burroughs from the Standards kept in the Exchequer at Westminster, subject nevertheless to such Regulations as the Parliament of Great Britain shall think fit.

Article 1: That the Laws concerning Regulation of Trade, Customs, and such Excises, to which Scotland is by virtue of this Treaty to be liable, be the same in Scotland, from and after the Union as in England; and that all other Laws, in use within the Kingdom of Scotland do after the Union, and notwithstanding thereof, remain in the same force as before (except such as are contrary to or inconsistent with this Treaty) but alterable by the Parliament of Great Britain, With this difference betwixt the Laws concerning publick right Policy, and Civil Government, and those which concern private right and the Laws which concern publick right Policy and Civil Government may be made the same throughout the whole United Kingdom; but that no alteration be made in

Laws which concern private Right, except for the evident utility of the subjects within Scotland.

Article 19: That the Court of Session or Colledge of Justice, do after the Union and notwithstanding thereof, remain in all time coming within Scotland as it is now constituted by the Laws of that Kingdom, and with the same Authority and Priviledges as before the Union; subject nevertheless to such Regulations for the better Administration of Justice as shall be made by the Parliament of Great Britain; And that hereafter none shall be named by Her Majesty or Her Royal Successors to be Ordinary Lords of Session but such who have served in the Colledge of Justice as Advocats or Principal Clerks of Session for the space of five years, or as Writers to the Signet for the space of ten years With this provision That no Writer to the Signet be capable to be admitted a Lord of the Session unless he undergo a private and publick Tryal on the Civil Law before the Faculty of Advocats and be found by them qualified for the said Office two years before he be named to be a Lord of the Session, yet so as the Qualifications made or to be made for capacitating persons to be named Ordinary Lords of Session may be altered by the Parliament of Great Britain.

And that the Court of Justiciary do also after the Union, and notwithstanding thereof remain in all time coming within Scotland, as it is now constituted by the Laws of that Kingdom, and with the same Authority and Priviledges as before the Union; subject nevertheless to such Regulations as shall be made by the Parliament of Great Britain, and without prejudice of other Rights of Justiciary:

And that all Admiralty Jurisdictions be under the Lord High Admirall or Commissioners for the Admiralty of

Great Britain for the time being; And that the Court of Admiralty now Established in Scotland be continued, And that all Reviews, Reductions or Suspensions of the Sentences in Maritime Cases competent to the Jurisdiction of that Court remain the the same manner after the Union as now in Scotland, until the Parliament of Great Britain shall make such Regulations and Alterations, as shall be judged expedient for the whole United Kingdom, so as there be alwayes continued in Scotland a Court of Admiralty such as in England, for determination of all Maritime Cases relating to private Rights in Scotland competent to the Jurisdiction of the Admiralty Court; subject nevertheless to such Regulations and Alterations as shall be thought proper to be made by the Parliament of Great Britain; And that the Heritable Rights of Admiralty and Vice-Admiralties in Scotland be reserved to the respective Proprietors as Rights of Property, subject nevertheless, as to the manner of Exercising such Heritable Rights to such Regualtions and Alterations as shall be thought proper to be made by the Parliament of Great Britain;

And that all other Courts now in being within the Kingdom of Scotland do remain, but subject to Alterations by the Parliament of Great Britain; And that all Inferior Courts within the said Limits do remain subordinate, as they are now to the Supream Courts of Justice within the same in all time coming;

And that no Causes in Scotland be cognoscible by the Courts of Chancery, Queens-Bench, Common-Pleas, or any other Court in Westminster-hall; And that the said Courts, or any other of the like nature after the Union, shall have no power to Cognosce, Review or Alter the Acts or Sentences of the Judicatures within Scotland, or stop the Execution of the same;

And that there be a Court of Exchequer in Scotland after the Union, for deciding Questions concerning the Revenues of Customs and Excises there, having the same power and authority in such cases, as the Court of Exchequer has in England And that the said Court of Exchequer in Scotland have power of passing Signatures, Gifts Tutories, and in other things as the Court of Exchequer in Scotland hath; And that the Court of Exchequer that now is in Scotland do remain, until a New Court of Exchequer be settled by the Parliament of Great Britain in Scotland after the Union;

And that after the Union the Queens Majesty and Her Royal Successors, may Continue a Privy Council in Scotland, for preserving of public Peace and Order, until the Parliament of Great Britain shall think fit to alter it or establish any other effectual method for that end.

Article 20: That all heritable Offices, Superiorities, heritable Jurisdictions, Offices for life, and Jurisdictions for life, be reserved to the Owners thereof, as Rights of Property, in the same manner as they are now enjoyed by the Laws of Scotland, notwithstanding of this Treaty.

Article 21: That the Rights and Privileges of the Royall Burroughs in Scotland as they now are, Do Remain entire after the Union, and notwithstanding thereof.

Article 22: That by virtue of this Treaty, Of the Peers of Scotland at the time of the Union 16 shall be the number to Sit and Vote in the House of Lords, and 45 the number of the Representatives of Scotland in the House of Commons of the Parliament of Great Britain; And that when Her Majesty Her Heirs or Successors, shall Declare Her or their pleasure for holding the first or any subsequent

Parliament of Great Britain until the Parliament of Great Britain shall make further provision therein, A Writ do issue under the Great Seal of the United Kingdom, Directed to the Privy Council of Scotland, Commanding them to Cause 16 Peers, who are to sit in the House of Lords to be Summoned to Parliament and 45 Members to be Elected to sit in the House of Commons of the Parliament of Great Britain according to the Agreement in the Treaty, in such manner as by a subsequent Act of this present Session of the Parliament of Scotland shall be settled; Which Act is hereby Declared to be as valid as if it were a part of and ingrossed in this Treaty:

And that the Names of the Persons so Summoned and Elected, shall be Returned by the Privy Council of Scotland into the Court from whence the said Writ did issue. And that if her Majesty, on or before the 1st day of May next, on which day the Union is to take place shall Declare under the Great Seal of England, That it is expedient, that the Lords of Parliament of England, and Commons of the present Parliament of England should be the Members of the respective Houses of the first Parliament of Great Britain for and on the part of England, then the said Lords of Parliament of England, and Commons of the present Parliament of England, shall be the members of the respective Houses of the first Parliament of Great Britain, for and on the part of England:

And Her Majesty may by Her Royal Proclamation under the Great Seal of Great Britain, appoint the said first Parliament of Great Britain to Meet at such time and place as Her Majesty shall think fit; which time shall not be less than 50 days after the date of such Proclamation; And the time and place of the Meeting of such Parliament being so appointed, a Writ shall be immediately issued under the Great Seal of Great Britain, directed to the Privy Council of Scotland, for the summoning the 16 Peers, and for Electing forty five Members, by whom Scotland is to be Represented in the Parliament of Great Britain:

And the Lords of Parliament of England, and the 16 Peers of Scotland, such 16 Peers being Summoned and Returned in the manner agreed by this Treaty; and the Members of the House of Commons of the said Parliament of England and the 45 Members for Scotland, such 45 Members being Elected and Returned in the manner agreed in this Treaty shall assemble and meet respectively in their respective houses of the Parliament of Great Britain, at such time and place as shall be so appointed by Her Majesty, and shall be the Two houses of the first Parliament of Great Britain, And that Parliament may Continue for such time only as the present Parliament of England might have Continued, if the Union of the Two Kingdoms had not been made, unless sooner Dissolved by Her Majesty;

And that every one of the Lords of Parliament of Great Britain, and every member of the House of Commons of the Parliament of Great Britain in the first and all succeeding Parliaments of Great Britain until the Parliament of Great Britain shall otherwayes Direct, shall take the respective Oaths, appointed to be taken in stead of the Oaths of Allegiance and Supremacy, by an Act of Parliament made in England in the first year of the Reign of the late King William and Queen Mary entituled An Act for the abrogating of the Oaths of Supremacy and Allegiance, and appointing other Oaths, and Make Subscribe and audibly Repeat the Declaration mentioned in an Act of Parliament made in England in the 30th year of the Reign of King Charles the Second entituled An Act for the more effectual preserving the Kings Person and Government by Disabling Papists from sitting in either House of Parliament, and shall take and subscribe the Oath mentioned in An Act of Parliament made in England, in the first year of Her Majesties Reign entituled An Act to Declare the Alterations in the Oath appointed to be taken by the Act Entituled An Act for the further security of His Majesties Person, and the Succession of the Crown in the Protestant Line, and for Extinguishing the Hopes of the pretended Prince of Wales, and all other pretenders and their open and secret Abettors, and for Declaring the Association to be determined, at such time, and in such manner as the Members of both Houses of Parliament of England are by the said respective Acts, directed to take, make and subscribe the same upon the penalties and disabilities in the said respective Acts contained.

And it is Declared and Agreed That these words This Realm, the Crown of this Realm, and the Queen of this Realm, mentioned in the Oaths and Declaration contained in the aforsaid Acts, which were intended to signify the Crown and Realm of England, shall be understood of the Crown and Realm of Great Britain, And that in that sense, the said Oaths and Declaration be taken and subscribed by the members of both Houses of the Parliament of Great Britain.

Article 23: That the foresaid 16 Peers of Scotland, mentioned in the last preceding Article, to sit in the House of Lords of the Parliament of Great Britain shall have all Priviledges of Parliament which the Peers of England now have, and which They or any Peers of Great Britain shall have after the Union, and particularly the Right of sitting upon the tryals of Peers: And in case of the tryal of any Peer in time of Adjournment or Prorogation of Parliament, the said 16 Peers shall be summoned in the same manner, and have the same powers and priviledges at such tryal, as any other Peers of Great Britain; And that in case any tryals of Peers shall hereafter happen when there is no Parliament in being, the 16 Peers of Scotland who sate in the last preceeding Parliament, shall be summoned in the same manner and have the same powers and privileges at such tryals as any other Peers of Great Britain;

And that all Peers of Scotland, and their successors to their Honours and Dignities, shall from and after the Union be Peers of Great Britain, and have Rank and Precedency next and immediately after the Peers of the like orders and degrees in England at the time of the Union, and before all Peers of Great Britain of the like orders and degrees, who may be Created after the Union, and shall be tryed as Peers of Great Britain, and shall Enjoy all Privileges of Peers, as fully as the Peers of England do now, or as they, or any other Peers of Great Britain may hereafter Enjoy the same except the Right and Privilege of sitting in the House of Lords and the Privileges depending thereon, and particularly the Right of sitting upon the tryals of Peers.

Article 24: That from and after the Union, there be One Great Seal for the United Kingdom of Great Britain, which shall be different from the Great Seal now used in either Kingdom; And that the Quartering the Arms and the Rank and Precedency of the Lyon King of Arms of the Kingdom of Scotland as may best suit the Union be left to Her Majesty: And that in the mean time the Great

Seal of England be used as the Great Seal of the United Kingdom, and that the Great Seal of the United Kingdom be used for Sealing Writs to Elect and Summon the Parliament of Great Britain and for sealing all Treaties with Forreign Princes and States, and all publick Acts Instruments and Orders of State which Concern the whole United Kingdom, and in all other matters relating to England, as the Great Seal of England is now used, and that a Seal in Scotland after the Union be alwayes kept and made use of in all things relating to private Rights or Grants, which have usually passed the Great Seal of Scotland, and which only concern Offices, Grants, Commissions, and private Rights within the Kingdom, And that until such Seal shall be appointed by Her Majesty the present Great Seal of Scotland shall be used for such purposes;

And that the Privy Seal, Signet, Casset, Signet of the Justiciary Court, Quarter Seal, and Seals of Courts now used in Scotland be Continued, but that the said Seals be altered and adapted to the state of the Union as Her Majesty shall think fit; And the said Seals, and all of them, and the Keepers of them, shall be subject to Regulations as the Parliament of Great Britain shall hereafter make:

And that the Crown, Scepter and Sword of State, the Records of Parliament, and all other Records, Rolls and Registers whatsoever, both publick and private generall and particular, and Warrands thereof Continue to be keeped as they are within that part of the United Kingdom now called Scotland, and that they shall so remain in all time coming, notwithstanding of the Union.

Article 25: That all Laws and Statutes in either Kingdom so far as they are contrary to, or inconsistent with the Terms of these Articles, or any of them, shall from and after the Union cease and become void, and shall be so declared to be by the respective Parliaments of the said Kingdoms.

THE UNION *with* IRELAND ACT, 1800

An Act for the Union of Great Britain and Ireland.

WHEREAS in pursuance of his Majesty's most gracious Recommendation to the two Houses of Parliament in Great Britain and Ireland respectively, to consider of such Measures as might best tend to strengthen and consolidate the Connection between the two Kingdoms, the two Houses of the Parliament of Great Britain and the two Houses of the Parliament of Ireland have severally agreed and resolved, that, in order to promote and secure the essential Interests of Great Britain and Ireland, and to consolidate the Strength, Power, and Resources of the British Empire, it will be advisable to concur in such Measures as may best tend to unite the two Kingdoms of Great Britain and Ireland into one Kingdom, in such Manner, and on such Terms and Conditions, as may be established by the Acts of the respective Parliaments of Great Britain and Ireland:

And whereas, in furtherance of the said Resolution, both Houses of the said two Parliaments respectively have likewise agreed upon certain Articles for effectuating and establishing the said Purposes, in the Tenor following:

Article 1: That it be the first Article of the Union of the Kingdoms of Great Britain and Ireland, that the said Kingdoms of Great Britain and Ireland shall, upon the first Day of January which shall be in the Year of our Lord one thousand eight hundred and one, and for ever after, be united into one Kingdom, by the Name of The United Kingdom of Great Britain and Ireland; and that the Royal

Stile and Titles appertaining to the Imperial Crown of the said United Kingdom and its Dependencies, and also the Ensigns, Armorial Flags and Banners thereof, shall be such as his Majesty, by his Royal Proclamation under the Great Seal of the United Kingdom, shall be pleased to appoint.

Article 2: That it be the second Article of Union, that the Succession to the Imperial Crown of the said United Kingdom, and of the Dominions thereunto belonging, shall continue limited and settled in the same Manner as the Succession to the Imperial Crown of the said Kingdoms of Great Britain and Ireland now stands limited and settled, according to the existing Laws, and to the Terms of Union between England and Scotland.

Article 3: That it be the third Article of Union, that the said United Kingdom be represented in one and the same Parliament, to be stiled The Parliament of the United Kingdom of Great Britain and Ireland.

Article 4: That it be the fourth Article of Union, that four Lords Spiritual of Ireland by Rotation of Sessions, and twenty-eight Lords Temporal of Ireland, elected for Life by the Peers of Ireland, shall be the Number to sit and vote on the Part of Ireland in the House of Lords of the Parliament of the United Kingdom; and one hundred Commoners (two for each County of Ireland, two for the City of Dublin, two for the City of Cork, one for the University of Trinity College, and one for each of the thirty-one most considerable Cities, Towns, and Boroughs), be the Number to sit and vote on the Part of Ireland in the House of Commons of the Parliament of the United Kingdom:

That such Act as shall be passed in the Parliament of

Ireland previous to the Union, to regulate the Mode by which the Lords Spiritual and Temporal, and the Commons, to serve in the Parliament of the United Kingdom on the Part of Ireland, shall be summoned and returned to the said Parliament, shall be considered as forming Part of the Treaty of Union, and shall be incorporated in the Acts of the respective Parliaments by which the said Union shall be ratified and established:

That all Questions touching the Rotation or Election of Lords Spiritual or Temporal of Ireland to sit in the Parliament of the United Kingdom, shall be decided by the House of Lords thereof; and whenever, by reason of an Equality of Votes in the Election of any such Lords Temporal, a complete Election shall not be made according to the true Intent of this Article, the Names of those Peers for whom such Equality of Votes shall be so given, shall be written on Pieces of Paper of a similar Form, and shall be put into a Glass, by the Clerk of the Parliaments at the Table of the House of Lords, whilst the House is sitting; and the Peer or Peers, whose Name or Names shall be first drawn out by the Clerk of the Parliaments, shall be deemed the Peer or Peers elected, as the Case may be:

That any Person holding any Peerage of Ireland now subsisting, or hereafter to be created, shall not thereby be disqualified from being elected to serve if he shall so think fit, or from serving or continuing to serve, if he shall so think fit, for any County, City, or Borough of Great Britain, in the House of Commons of the United Kingdom, unless he shall have been previously elected as above, to sit in the House of Lords of the United Kingdom; but that so long as such Peer of Ireland shall so continue to be a Member of the House of Commons, he shall not be entitled to the Privilege of Peerage, nor be capable of being elected to serve as a Peer on the Part of Ireland, or of voting at any such Election; and that he shall be liable to be sued, indicted, proceeded against, and tried as a Commoner, for any Offence with which he may be charged:

That it shall be lawful for his Majesty, his Heirs and Successors, to create Peers of that Part of the United Kingdom called Ireland, and to make Promotions in the Peerage thereof after the Union; provided that no new Creation of any such Peers shall take place after the Union until three of the Peerages of Ireland, which shall have been existing at the Time of the Union, shall have become extinct; and upon such Extinction of three Peerages, that it shall be lawful for his Majesty, his Heirs and Successors, to create one Peer of that Part of the United Kingdom called Ireland; and in like Manner so often as three Peerages of that Part of the United Kingdom called Ireland shall become extinct, it shall be lawful for his Majesty, his Heirs and Successors, to create one other Peer of the said Part of the United Kingdom; and if it shall happen that the Peers of that Part of the United Kingdom called Ireland, shall, by Extinction of Peerages or otherwise, be reduced to the Number of One Hundred, exclusive of all such Peers of that Part of the United Kingdom called Ireland, as shall hold any Peerage of Great Britain subsisting at the Time of the Union, or of the United Kingdom created since the Union, by which such Peers shall be entitled to an Hereditary Seat in the House of Lords of the United Kingdom, then and in that Case it shall and may be lawful for his Majesty, his Heirs and Successors, to create one Peer of that Part of the United Kingdom called Ireland as often as any one of such One Hundred Peerages shall fail by Extinction, or as often as any one Peer of that Part of the United Kingdom called Ireland shall become entitled, by Descent or Creation, to an Hereditary Seat in the House of Lords of the United Kingdom; it being the true Intent and Meaning of this Article, that at all Times after the Union it shall and may be lawful for his Majesty, his Heirs and Successors, to keep up the Peerage of that Part of the United Kingdom called Ireland to the Number of one hundred, over and above the Number of such of the said Peers as shall be entitled, by Descent or Creation, to an Hereditary Seat in the House of Lords of the United Kingdom:

That if any Peerage shall at any Time be in Abeyance, such Peerage shall be deemed and taken as an existing Peerage; and no Peerage shall be deemed extinct, unless on Default of Claimants to the Inheritance of such Peerage for the Space of one Year from the Death of the Person who shall have been last possessed thereof; and if no Claim shall be made to the Inheritance of such Peerage, in such Form and Manner as may from Time to Time be prescribed by the House of Lords of the United Kingdom, before the Expiration of the said Period of a Year, then and in that Case such Peerage shall be deemed extinct; provided that nothing herein shall exclude any Person from afterwards putting in a Claim to the Peerage so deemed extinct; and if such Claim shall be allowed as valid, by Judgment of the House of Lords of the United Kingdom, reported to his Majesty, such Peerage shall be considered as revived; and in case any new Creation of a Peerage of that Part of the United Kingdom called Ireland, shall have taken place in the Interval, in consequence of the supposed Extinction of such Peerage, then no new Right of Creation shall accrue to his Majesty, his Heirs or Successors, in consequence of the next Extinction which shall take place of any Peerage of that Part of the

United Kingdom called Ireland

That all Questions touching the Election of Members to sit on the Part of Ireland in the House of Commons of the United Kingdom shall be heard and decided in the same Manner as Questions touching such Elections in Great Britain now are, or at any Time hereafter shall by Law be heard and decided; subject nevertheless to such particular Regulations in respect of Ireland, as, from local Circumstances, the Parliament of the United Kingdom may from Time to Time deem expedient:

That the Qualifications in respect of Property of the Members elected on the Part of Ireland to sit in the House of Commons of the United Kingdom, shall be respectively the same as are now provided by Law in the Case of Elections for Counties and Cities and Boroughs respectively in that Part of Great Britain called England, unless any other Provision shall hereafter be made in that respect by Act of Parliament of the United Kingdom:

That when his Majesty, his Heirs or Successors, shall declare his, her, or their Pleasure for holding the first or any subsequent Parliament of the United Kingdom, a Proclamation shall issue, under the Great Seal of the United Kingdom, to cause the Lords Spiritual and Temporal, and Commons, who are to serve in the Parliament thereof on the Part of Ireland, to be retuned in such Manner as by any Act of this present Session of the Parliament of Ireland shall be provided; and that the Lords Spiritual and Temporal and Commons of Great Britain shall, together with the Lords Spiritual and Temporal and Commons so returned as aforesaid on the Part of Ireland, constitute the two Houses of the Parliament of the United Kingdom:

That if his Majesty, on or before the first Day of January one thousand eight hundred and one, on which Day the Union is to take place, shall declare, under the Great Seal of Great Britain, that it is expedient that the Lords and Commons of the present Parliament of Great Britain should be the Members of the respective Houses of the first Parliament of the United Kingdom on the Part of Great Britain; then the said Lords and Commons of the present Parliament of Great Britain shall accordingly be the Members of the respective Houses of the first Parliament of the United Kingdom on the Part of Great Britain; and they, together with the Lords Spiritual and Temporal and Commons, so summoned and returned as above on the Part of Ireland, shall be the Lords Spiritual and Temporal and Commons of the first Parliament of the United Kingdom; and such first Parliament may (in that Case) if not sooner dissolved, continue to sit so long as the present Parliament of Great Britain may now by Law continue to sit, if not sooner dissolved: Provided always, That until an Act shall have passed in the Parliament of the United Kingdom, providing in what Cases Persons holding Offices or Places of Profit under the Crown of Ireland, shall be incapable of being Members of the House of Commons of the Parliament of the United Kingdom, no greater Number of Members than twenty, holding such Offices or Places as aforesaid, shall be capable of sitting in the said House of Commons of the Parliament of the United Kingdom; and if such a Number of Members shall be returned to serve in the said House as to make the whole Number of Members of the said House holding such Offices or Places as aforesaid more than twenty, then and in such Case the Seats or Places of such Members as shall have last accepted such Offices or Places shall be vacated, at the Option of such Members, so as to reduce the Number of Members holding such Offices or Places to the Number of twenty; and no Person holding any such Office or Place shall be capable of being elected or of sitting in the said House, while there are twenty Persons holding such Offices or Places sitting in the said House; and that every one of the Lords of Parliament of the United Kingdom, and every Member of the House of Commons of the United Kingdom, in the first and all succeeding Parliaments, shall, until the Parliament of the United Kingdom shall otherwise provide, take the Oaths, and make and subscribe the Declaration, and take and subscribe the Oath now by Law enjoined to be taken, made, and subscribed by the Lords and Commons of the Parliament of Great Britain:

That the Lords of Parliament on the Part of Ireland, in the House of Lords of the United Kingdom, shall at all Times have the same Privileges of Parliament which shall belong to the Lords of Parliament on the Part of Great Britain; and the Lords Spiritual and Temporal respectively on the Part of Ireland shall at all Times have the same Rights in respect of their sitting and voting upon the Trial of Peers, as the Lords Spiritual and Temporal respectively on the Part of Great Britain; and that all Lords Spiritual of Ireland shall have Rank and Precedency next and immediately after the Lords Spiritual of the same Rank and Degree of Great Britain, and shall enjoy all Privileges as fully as the Lords Spiritual of Great Britain do now or may hereafter enjoy the same (the Right and Privilege of sitting in the House of Lords, and the Privileges depending thereon, and particularly the Right of sitting on the Trial of Peers, excepted); and that the Persons holding any temporal Peerages of Ireland, existing at the Time of the Union, shall, from and after the Union, have Rank and Precedency next and immediately after all the Persons holding Peerage of the like Orders and Degrees in Great Britain, subsisting at the Time of the Union; and that all Peerages of Ireland created after the Union shall have Rank and Precedency with the Peerages of the United Kingdom, so created, according to the Dates of their Creations: and that all Peerages both of Great Britain and Ireland, now subsisting or hereafter to be created, shall in all other Respects, from the Date of the Union, be considered as Peerages of the United Kingdom; and that the Peers of Ireland shall, as Peers of the United Kingdom, be sued and tried as Peers, except as aforesaid, and shall enjoy all Privileges of Peers as fully as the Peers of Great Britain; the Right and Privilege of sitting in the House of Lords, and the Privileges depending thereon, and the Right of sitting on the Time of Peers, only excepted:

Article 5: That it be the Fifth Article of Union, That the Churches of England and Ireland, as now by Law established, be united into one Protestant Episcopal Church, to be called, The United Church of England and Ireland; and that the Doctrine, Worship, Discipline, and Government of the said United Church shall be, and shall remain in full force for ever, as the same are now by Law established for the Church of England; and that the Continuance and Preservation of the said United Church, as the established Church of England and Ireland, shall be deemed and taken to be an essential and fundamental Part of the Union; and that in like Manner the Doctrine, Worship, Discipline, and Government of the Church of Scotland, shall remain and be preserved as the same are now established by Law, and by the Acts for the Union of the two Kingdoms of England and Scotland.

Article 6: That it be the Sixth Article of Union, That his

Majesty's Subjects of Great Britain and Ireland shall, from and after the first Day of January one thousand eight hundred and one, be entitled to the same Privileges, and be on the same Footing, as to Encouragements and Bounties on the like Articles being the Growth, Produce, or Manufacture of either Country respectively, and generally in respect of Trade and Navigation in all Ports and Places in the United Kingdom and its Dependencies; and that in all Treaties made by his Majesty, his Heirs and Successors, with any Foreign Power, his Majesty's Subjects of Ireland shall have the same Privileges, and be on the same Footing as his Majesty's Subjects of Great Britain:

That, from the first Day of January one thousand eight hundred and one, all Prohibitions and Bounties on the Export of Articles, the Growth, Produce, or Manufacture of either Country, to the other, shall cease and determine; and that the said Articles shall thenceforth be exported from one Country to the other, without Duty or Bounty on such Export:

That all Articles, the Growth, Produce, or Manufacture of either Country, (not herein-after enumerated as subject to specific Duties) shall from thenceforth be imported into each Country from the other, free from Duty, other than such Countervailing Duties on the several Articles enumerated in the Schedule Number One A. and B. hereunto annexed, as are therein specified, or to such other Countervailing Duties as shall hereafter be imposed by the Parliament of the United Kingdom, in the Manner herein-after provided; and that, for the Period of twenty Years from the Union, the Articles enumerated in the Schedule Number Two hereunto annexed, shall be subject, on Importation into each Country from the other, to the Duties specified in the said Schedule Number Two; and the Woollen Manufactures, known by the Names of Old and New Drapery, shall pay, on Importation into each Country from the other, the Duties now payable on Importation into Ireland: Salt and Hops, on Importation into Ireland from Great Britain, Duties not exceeding those which are now paid on Importation into Ireland; and Coals, on Importation into Ireland from Great Britain, shall be subject to Burthens not exceeding those to which they are now subject:

That Callicoes and Muslins shall, on their Importation into either Country from the other, be subject and liable to the Duties now payable on the same on the Importation thereof from Great Britain into Ireland, until the fifth Day of January one thousand eight hundred and eight; and from and after the said Day, the said Duties shall be annually reduced, by equal Proportions as near as may be in each Year, so as that the said Duties shall stand at ten per Centum from and after the fifth Day of January one thousand eight hundred and sixteen, until the fifth Day of January one thousand eight hundred and twenty-one:

And that Cotton Yarn and Cotton Twist shall, on their Importation into either Country from the other, be subject and liable to the Duties now payable upon the same on the Importation thereof from Great Britain into Ireland, until the fifth Day of January one thousand eight hundred and eight; and from and after the said Day, the said Duties shall be annually reduced, by equal Proportions as near as may be in each Year, so as that all Duties shall cease on the said Articles from and after the fifth Day of January one thousand eight hundred and sixteen:

That any Articles of the Growth, Produce, or Manufacture

of either Country, which are or may be subject to Internal Duty, or to Duty on the Materials of which they are composed, may be made subject, on their Importation into each Country respectively from the other, to such Countervailing Duty as shall appear to be just and reasonable in respect of such Internal Duty or Duties on the Materials; and that for the said Purposes the Articles specified in the said Schedule Number One, A. and B. shall be subject to the Duties set forth therein, liable to be taken off, diminished, or increased, in the Manner herein specified; and that upon the Export of the said Articles from each Country to the other respectively, a Drawback shall be given equal in Amount to the Countervailing Duty payable on such Articles on the Import thereof into the same Country from the other; and that in like Manner in future it shall be competent to the United Parliament to impose any new or additional Countervailing Duties, or to take off or diminish such existing Countervailing Duties as may appear, on like Principles, to be just and reasonable in respect of any future or additional Internal Duty on any Article of the Growth, Produce, or Manufacture of either Country, or of any new or additional Duty on any Materials of which such Article may be composed, or of any Abatement of Duty on the same; and that when any such new or additional Countervailing Duty shall be so imposed on the Import of any Article into either Country from the other, a Drawback, equal in Amount to such Countervailing Duty, shall be given in like Manner on the Export of every such Article respectively from the same Country to the other:

That all Articles, the Growth, Produce, or Manufacture of either Country, when exported through the other, shall in all Cases be exported subject to the same Charges as if they had been exported directly from the Country of which they were the Growth, Produce, or Manufacture:

That all Duty charged on the Import of Foreign or Colonial Goods into either Country shall, on their Export to the other, be either drawn back, or the Amount, (if any be retained,) shall be placed to the Credit of the Country to which they shall be so exported, so long as the Expenditure of the United Kingdom shall be defrayed by proportional Contributions: Provided always, That nothing herein shall extend to take away any Duty, Bounty, or Prohibition, which exists with respect to Corn, Meal, Malt, Flour, or Biscuit; but that all Duties, Bounties, or Prohibitions, on the said Articles, may be regulated, varied, or repealed, from Time to Time, as the United Parliament shall deem expedient.

Article 7: That it be the seventh Article of Union, that the Charge arising from the Payment of the Interest, and the Sinking Fund for the Reduction of the Principal, of the Debt incurred in either Kingdom before the Union, shall continue to be separately defrayed by Great Britain and Ireland respectively, except as hereinafter provided: That for the Space of twenty Years after the Union shall take place, the Contribution of Great Britain and Ireland respectively, towards the Expenditure of the United Kingdom in each Year, shall be defrayed in the Proportion of fifteen Parts for Great Britain and two Parts for Ireland; and that at the Expiration of the said twenty Years, the future Expenditure of the United Kingdom (other than the Interest and Charges of the Debt to which either Country shall be separately liable) shall be defrayed in such Proportion as the Parliament of the United Kingdom shall deem just and reasonable upon a Comparison of the real Value of the Exports and Imports of the respective Countries, upon an Average of the three Years next preceding the Period of Revision: or on a Comparison of the Value of the Quantities of the following Articles consumed within the respective Countries, on a similar Average, videlicet, Beer, Spirits, Sugar, Wine, Tea, Tobacco, and Malt; or according to the aggregate Proportion resulting from both these Considerations combined; or on a Comparison of the Amount of Income in each Country, estimated from the Produce for the same Period of a general Tax, if such shall have been imposed on the same Descriptions of Income in both Countries; and that the Parliament of the United Kingdom shall afterwards proceed in like Manner to revise and fix the said Proportions according to the same Rules, or any of them, at Periods not more distant than twenty years, nor less than seven Years from each other; unless, previous to any such Period, the Parliament of the United Kingdom shall have declared, as herein-after provided, that the Expenditure of the United Kingdom shall be defrayed indiscriminately, by equal Taxes imposed on the like Articles in both Countries. That, for the defraying the said Expenditure according to the Rules above laid down, the Revenues of Ireland shall hereafter constitute a Consolidated Fund, which shall be charged, in the first Instance, with the Interest of the Debt of Ireland, and with the Sinking Fund, applicable to the Reduction of the said Debt, and the Remainder shall be applied towards defraying the Proportion of the Expenditure of the United Kingdom, to which Ireland may be liable in each Year: That the Proportion of Contribution to which Great Britain and Ireland will be liable, shall be raised by such Taxes in each Country respectively, as the Parliament of the United Kingdom shall from Time to Time deem fit: Provided always, That in regulating the Taxes in each Country, by which their respective Proportions shall be levied, no Article in Ireland shall be made liable to any new or additional Duty, by which the whole Amount of Duty payable thereon would exceed the Amount which shall be thereafter payable in England on the like Article: That, if at the End of any Year any Surplus shall accrue from the Revenues of Ireland, after defraying the Interest, Sinking Fund, and proportional Contribution and separate Charges to which the said Country shall then be liable, Taxes shall be taken off to the Amount of such Surplus, or the Surplus shall be applied by the Parliament of the United Kingdom to local Purposes in Ireland, or to make good any Deficiency which may arise in the Revenues of Ireland in Time of Peace, or be invested, by the Commissioners of the National Debt of Ireland, in the Funds, to accumulate for the Benefit of Ireland at Compound Interest, in case of the Contribution of Ireland in Time of War; provided that the Surplus so to accumulate shall at no future Period be suffered to exceed the Sum of five Millions: That all Monies to be raised after the Union, by Loan, in Peace or War, for the Service of the United Kingdom by the Parliament thereof, shall be considered to be a joint Debt, and the Charges thereof shall be borne by the respective Countries in the Proportion of their respective Contributions; provided that, if at any Time, in raising their respective Contributions hereby fixed for each Country, the Parliament of the United Kingdom shall judge it fit to raise a greater Proportion of such respective Contributions in one Country within the Year than in the other, or to set apart a greater Proportion Sinking Fund for the Liquidation of the Whole or any Part of the Loan raised on account of the one Country than of that raised on account of the other Country, then such Part of the said Loan, for the Liquidation of which different Provisions shall have been made for the respective Countries, shall be kept distinct, and shall be borne by each separately, and only that Part of the said Loan be deemed Joint and Common, for the Reduction of which the respective Countries shall have made Provision in the Proportion of their respective Contributions: That, if at any future Day the separate Debt of each Country respectively shall have been liquidated, or, if the Values of their respective Debts (estimated according to the Amount of the Interest and Annuities attending the same, and of the Sinking Fund applicable to the Reduction thereof, and to the Period within which the whole Capital of such Debt shall appear to be redeemable by such Sinking Fund) shall be to each other in the same Proportion with the respective Contributions of each Country respectively; or if the Amount by which the Value of the larger of such Debts shall vary from such Proportion, shall not exceed one hundredth Part of the said Value; and if it shall appear to the Parliament of the United Kingdom, that the respective Circumstances of the two Countries will thenceforth admit of their contributing indiscriminately, by equal Taxes imposed on the same Articles in each, to the future Expenditure of the United Kingdom, it shall be competent to the Parliament of the United Kingdom to declare, that all future Expence thenceforth to be incurred, together with the Interest and Charges of all joint Debts contracted previous to such Declaration, shall be to defrayed indiscriminately by equal Taxes imposed on the same Articles in each Country, and thenceforth from Time to Time, as Circumstances may require, to impose and apply such Taxes accordingly, subject only to such particular Exemptions or Abatements in Ireland, and in that Part of Great Britain called Scotland, as Circumstances may appear from Time to Time to demand: That, from the Period of such Declaration, it shall no longer be necessary to regulate the Contribution of the two Countries towards the future Expenditure of the United Kingdom, according to any specifick Proportion, or according to any of the Rules herein-before prescribed: Provided nevertheless, that the Interest or Charges which may remain on account of any Part of the separate Debt with which either Country shall be chargeable, and which shall not be liquidated or consolidated proportionably as above, shall, until extinguished, continue to be defrayed by separate Taxes in each Country: That a Sum, not less than the Sum which has been granted by the Parliament of Ireland on the Average of six Years immediately preceding the first Day of January in the Year of our Lord one thousand eight hundred, in Premiums for the internal Encouragement of Agriculture or Manufactures, or for the maintaining Institutions for pious and charitable Purposes, shall be applied, for the Period of twenty Years after the Union, to such local Purposes in Ireland, in such Manner as the Parliament of the United Kingdom shall direct: That, from and after the first Day of January one thousand eight hundred and one, all Publick Revenue arising to the United Kingdom from the territorial Dependencies thereof, and applied to the General Expenditure of the United Kingdom, shall be so applied in the Proportions of the respective Contributions of the two Countries:

Article 8: That it be the eighth Article of Union, That all Laws in force at the Time of the Union, and all the Courts of Civil and Ecclesiastical Jurisdiction within the respective Kingdoms, shall remain as now by Law established within the same; subject only to such Alterations and Regulations from Time to Time as

Circumstances may appear to the Parliament of the United Kingdom to require; provided that all Writs of Error and Appeals depending at the Time of the Union or hereafter to be brought, and which might now be finally decided by the House of Lords of either Kingdom, shall, from and after the Union, be finally decided by the House of Lords of the United Kingdom; and provided, that, from and after the Union, there shall remain in Ireland an Instance Court of Admiralty, for the Determination of Causes, Civil and Maritime only, and that the Appeal from Sentences of the said Court shall be to his Majesty's Delegates in his Court of Chancery in that Part of the United Kingdom called Ireland; and that all Laws at present in force in either Kingdom, which shall be contrary to any of the Provisions which may be enacted by any Act for carrying these Articles into Effect, be from and after the Union repealed.

And whereas the said Articles having, by Address of the respective Houses of Parliament in Great Britain and Ireland, been humbly laid before his Majesty, his Majesty has been graciously pleased to approve the same; and to recommend it to his two Houses of Parliament in Great Britain and Ireland to consider of such Measures as may be necessary for giving Effect to the said Articles: In order, therefore, to give full Effect and Validity to the same, be it enacted by the King's most excellent Majesty, by and with the Advice and Consent of the Lords Spiritual and Temporal, and Commons, in this present Parliament assembled, and by the Authority of the same, That, the said foregoing recited Articles, each and every one of them, according to the true Import and Tenor thereof, be ratified, confirmed, and approved, and be and they are hereby declare to be, the Articles of the Union of Great Britain and Ireland, and the same shall be in force and have effect for ever, from the first Day of January which shall be in the Year of our Lord one thousand eight hundred and one; provided that before that Period an Act shall have been passed by the Parliament of Ireland, for carrying into effect, in the like Manner, the said foregoing recited Articles.

II. And whereas an Act, intituled, An Act to regulate the Mode by which the Lords Spiritual and Temporal, and the Commons, to serve in the Parliament of the United Kingdom on the Part of Ireland, shall be summoned and returned to the said Parliament, has been passed by the Parliament of Ireland; the Tenor whereof is as follows: 'An Act to regulate the Mode by which the Lords Spiritual and Temporal, and the Commons, to serve in the Parliament of the United Kingdom on the Part of Ireland, shall be summoned and returned to the said Parliament. Whereas it is agreed by the fourth Article of Union, That four Lords Spiritual of Ireland, by Rotation of Sessions, and twenty-eight Lords Temporal of Ireland, elected for Life by the Peers of Ireland, shall be the Number to sit and vote on the Part of Ireland in the House of Lords of the Parliament of the United Kingdom, and one hundred Commoners (two for each County of Ireland, two for the City of Dublin, two for the City of Cork, one for the College of the Holy Trinity of Dublin, and one for each of the thirty-one considerable Cities, Towns, and Boroughs) be the Number to sit and vote on the Part of Ireland in the House of Commons of the Parliament or the United Kingdom; be it enacted by the King's most Excellent Majesty, by and with the Advice and Consent of the Lords Spiritual and Temporal, and Commons, in this present Parliament assembled, and by Authority of the same, That the said four Lords Spiritual shall be taken from among the Lords Spiritual of Ireland in the Manner following; that is to say, That one of the four Archbishops of Ireland, and three of the eighteen Bishops of Ireland, shall sit in the House of Lords of the United Parliament in each Session thereof, the said Right of sitting being regulated as between the said Archbishops respectively by a Rotation among the Archiepiscopal Sees from Session to Session, and in like Manner that of the Bishops by a like Rotation among the Episcopal Sees: That the Primate of all Ireland for the Time being shall sit in the first Session of the Parliament of the United Kingdom, the Archbishop of Dublin for the Time being in the Second, the Archbishop of Cashel for the Time being in the third, the Archbishop of Tuam for the Time being in the fourth; and so by Rotation of Sessions for ever, such Rotation to proceed regularly and without Interruption from Session to Session notwithstanding any Dissolution or Expiration of Parliament: That three suffragan Bishops shall in like Manner sit according to their Rotation of Sees from Session to Session in the following Order; the Lord Bishop of Meath, the Lord Bishop of Kildare, the Lord Bishop of Derry, in the first Session of the Parliament of the United Kingdom; the Lord Bishop of Raphoe, the Lord Bishop of Limerick, Ardfert, and Aghadoe, the Lord Bishop of Dromore, in the second Session of the Parliament of the United Kingdom; the Lord Bishop of Elphin, the Lord Bishop of Down and Connor, the Lord Bishop of Waterford and Lismore, in the third Session of the Parliament of the United Kingdom; the Lord Bishop of Leighlin and Ferns, the Lord Bishop of Cloyne, the Lord Bishop of Cork and Ross in the, fourth Session of the Parliament of the United Kingdom; the Lord Bishop of Killaloe and Kilfenora, the Lord Bishop of Kitmore, the Lord Bishop of Clogher, in the fifth Session of the Parliament of the United Kingdom; the Lord Bishop of Ossory, the Lord. Bishop of Killala and Achonry, the Lord Bishop of Clonfert and Kilmacduagh, in the sixth Session of the Parliament of the United Kingdom; the said Rotation to be nevertheless subject to such Variation therefrom from Time to Time as is herein-after provided: That the said twenty-eight Lords Temporal shall be chosen by all the Temporal Peers of Ireland in the Manner herein-after provided; that each of the said Lords Temporal so chosen shall be entitled to sit in the House of Lords of the Parliament of the United Kingdom during his Life; and in case of his Death, or forfeiture of any of the said Lords Temporal, the Temporal Peers of Ireland shall, in the Manner herein-after provided, choose another Peer out of their own Number to supply the Place so vacant. And be it enacted, That of the one hundred Commoners to sit on the Part of Ireland in the United Parliament, sixty-four shall be chosen for the Counties, and thirty-six for the following Cities and Boroughs, videlicet; For each County of Ireland two; for the City of Dublin two; for the City of Cork two; for the College of the Holy Trinity of Dublin one; for the City of Waterford one; for the City of Limerick one; for the Borough of Belfast one; for the County and Town of Drogheda one; for the County and Town of Carrickfergus one; for the Borough of Newry one, for the City of Kilkenny one; for the City of Londonderry one; for the Town of Galway one; for the Borough of Clonmell one; for the Town of Wexford one; for the Town of Youghall one; for the Town of Bandon Bridge one; for the Borough of Armagh one; for the Borough of Dundalk one; for the Town of Kinsale one; for the Borough of Lisburne one; for the Borough of Sligo one; for the Borough of Catherlough one; for the

Borough of Ennis one; for the Borough of Dungarvan one; for the Borough of Downpatrick one; for the Borough of Colraine one; for the Town of Mallow one; for the Borough of Athlone one; for the Town of New Ross one; for the Borough of Tralee one; for the City of Cashel one; for the Borough of Dungannon one; for the Borough of Portarlington one; for the Borough of Enniskillen one. And be it enacted, That in case of the summoning of a new Parliament, or if the Seat of any of the said Commoners shall become vacant by Death or otherwise, then the said Counties, Cities or Boroughs, or any of them, as the Case may be, shall proceed to a new Election; and that all the other Towns, Cities, Corporations, or Boroughs, other than the aforesaid, shall cease to elect Representatives to serve in Parliament; and no meeting shall at any Time hereafter be summoned, called, convened, or held, for the Purpose of electing any Person or Persons to serve or act, or be considered, as Representative or Representatives of any other Place, Town, City, Corporation, or Borough, other than the aforesaid, or as Representative or Representatives of the Freemen, Freeholders, Householders, or Inhabitants thereof, either in the Parliament of the United Kingdom or elsewhere, (unless it shall hereafter be otherwise provided by the Parliament of the United Kingdom); and every Person summoning, calling, or holding such a meeting or Assembly, or taking any part in any such Election or pretended Election, shall, being duly thereof convicted, incur and suffer the Pains and Penalties ordained and provided by the Statute of Provision and Præmunire, made in the sixteenth Year of the Reign of Richard the Second. For the due Election of the Persons to be chosen to sit in the respective Houses of the Parliament of the United Kingdom on the Part of Ireland, be it enacted, That on the Day following that on which the Act for establishing the Union shall have received the Royal Assent, the Primate of all Ireland, the Lord Bishop of Meath, the Lord Bishop of Kildare, and the Lord Bishop of Derry shall be and they are hereby declared to be the Representatives of the Lords Spiritual of Ireland in the Parliament of the United Kingdom, for the first Session thereof; and that the Temporal Peers of Ireland shall assemble at Twelve of the Clock on the same Day as aforesaid, in the now accustomed Place of Meeting of the House of Lords of Ireland, and shall then and there proceed to elect twenty-eight Lords Temporal to represent the Peerage of Ireland in the Parliament of the United Kingdom, in the following Manner; that is to say, the Names of the Peers shall be called over according to their Rank, by the Clerk of the Crown, or his Deputy, who shall then and there attend for that Purpose; and each of the said Peers, who previous to the said Day, and in the present Parliament shall have actually taken his Seat in the House of Lords of Ireland, and who shall there have taken the Oaths, and signed the Declaration, which are or shall be by Law required to be taken and signed by the Lords of the Parliament of Ireland before they can sit and vote in the Parliament hereof, shall, when his Name is called, deliver, either by himself or by his Proxy, (the Name of such Proxy having been previously entered in the Books of the House of Lords of Ireland, according to the present Forms and Usages thereof,) to the Clerk of the Crown or his Deputy, (who shall then and there attend for that Purpose,) a List of twenty-eight of the Peers of Ireland; and the Clerk of the Crown or his Deputy shall then and there publickly read the said Lists, and shall then and there cast up the said Lists, and publickly declare the Names of the twenty-eight Lords who shall be chosen by the Majority of Votes in the said Lists, and shall make a Return of the said Names to the House of Lords of the first Parliament of the United Kingdom; and the Lords so chosen by the Majority of Votes in the said Lists shall, during their respective Lives sit as Representatives of the Peers of Ireland in the House of Lords of the United Kingdom, and be entitled to receive Writs of Summons to that and every succeeding Parliament; and in case a complete Election shall not be made of the whole Number of twenty-eight Peers, by reason of an Equality of Votes, the Clerk of the Crown shall return such Number in favour of whom a complete Election shall have been made in one List, and in a second List shall return the Names of those Peers who shall have an Equality of Votes, but in favour of whom, by reason of such Equality, a complete Election shall not have been made and the Names of the Peers in the second List, for whom an equal Number of Votes shall have been so given, shall be written on Pieces of Paper of a similar Form, and shall be put into a Glass by the Clerk of the Parliament of the United Kingdom, at the Table of the House of Lords thereof, whilst the House is sitting, and the Peer whose Name shall be first drawn out by the Clerk of the Parliament, shall be deemed the Peer elected; and so successively as often as the Case may require; and whenever the Seat or any of the twenty-eight Lords Temporal so elected shall be vacated by Decease or Forfeiture, the Chancellor, the Keeper or Commissioners of the Great Seal of the United Kingdom for the Time being, upon receiving a Certificate under the Hand and Seal of any two Lords Temporal of the Parliament of the United Kingdom, certifying the Decease of such Peer, or on View of the Record of Attainder of such Peer, shall direct a Writ to be issued under the Great Seal of the United Kingdom, to the Chancellor, the Keeper or Commissioners of the Great Seal of Ireland for the time being, directing him or them to cause Writs to be issued, by the Clerk of the Crown in Ireland, to every Temporal Peer of Ireland, who shall have sat and voted in the House of Lords of Ireland before the Union, or whose Right to sit and vote therein, or to vote at such Elections, shall, on Claim made on his Behalf, have been admitted by the House of Lords of Ireland before the Union, or after the Union by the House of Lords of the United Kingdom; and Notice shall forthwith be published by the said Clerk of the Crown, in the London and Dublin Gazettes, of the issuing of such Writs, and of the Names and Titles of all the Peers to whom the same are directed; and to the said Writs there shall be annexed a Form of Return thereof, in which a Blank shall be left for the Peer to be elected, and the said Writs shall enjoin each Peer, within fifty-two Days from the Teste of the Writ, to return the same into the Crown Office of Ireland with the Blank filled up, by inserting the Name of the Peer for whom he shall vote, as the Peer to succeed to the vacancy made by Demise or Forfeiture as aforesaid; and the said Writs and Returns shall be bipartite, so as that the Name of the Peer to be chosen shall be written twice, that is, once on each part of such Writ and Return, and so as that each Part may also be subscribed by the Peer to whom the same shall be directed, and likewise be sealed with his Seal of Arms; and one Part of the said Writs and Returns so filled up, subscribed and sealed as above, shall remain of the Record in the Crown Office of Ireland, and the other Part shall be certified by the Clerk of the Crown to the Clerk of the Parliament of the United Kingdom; and no Peer of Ireland, except such as shall have been elected as

Representative Peers on the Part of Ireland in the House of Lords of the United Kingdom, and shall have taken the Oaths, and signed the Declaration prescribed by Law, shall, under pain of suffering such Punishment as the House of Lords of the United Kingdom may award and adjudge, make a Return to such Writ, unless he shall, after the issuing thereof, and before the Day on which the Writ is returnable, have taken the Oaths and signed the Declaration which are or shall be by Law required to be taken and signed by the Lords of the United Kingdom, before they can sit and vote in the Parliament thereof; which oaths and Declaration shall be either taken and subscribed in the Court of Chancery of Ireland, or before one of his Majesty's Justices of the Peace of that Part of the United Kingdom called Ireland; a certificate whereof, signed by such Justices of the Peace, or by the Registrar of the said Court of Chancery, shall be transmitted by such Peer with the Return, and shall be annexed to that Part thereof remaining as record in the Crown Office of Ireland; and the Clerk of the Crown shall forthwith after the Return Day of the Writs, cause to he published in the London and Dublin Gazettes, a Notice of the Name of the person chosen by the Majority of Votes; and the Peer so chosen shall, during his life, be one of the Peers to sit and vote on the Part of Ireland in the House of Lords of the United Kingdom; and in case the Votes shall be equal, the Names of such Persons who have an equal Number of Votes in their Favour, shall be written on Pieces of Paper of a similar Form, and shall be put into a Glass by the Clerk of the Parliament of the United Kingdom, at the Table of the House of Lords, whilst the House is sitting, and the Peer whose Name shall be first drawn out by the Clerk of the Parliament shall be deemed the Peer elected, And be it enacted, That in case any Lord Spiritual, being a Temporal Peer of the United Kingdom, or being a Temporal Peer of that Part of the United Kingdom called Ireland, shall be chosen by the Lords Temporal to be one of the Representatives of the Lords Temporal, in every such Case, during the Life of such Spiritual Peer being a Temporal Peer of the United Kingdom, or being a Temporal Peer of that Part of the United Kingdom called Ireland, so chosen to represent the Lords Temporal, the Rotation of Representation of the Spiritual Lords shall proceed to the next Spiritual Lord, without regard to such Spiritual Lord so chosen a temporal Peer, that is to say, if such Spiritual Lord shall be an Archbishop, then the Rotation shall proceed to the Archbishop whose See is next in Rotation, and if such Spiritual Lord shall be a suffragan Bishop, then the Rotation shall proceed to the suffragan Bishop whose See is next in Rotation. And whereas by the said fourth Article of Union it is agreed, that, if his Majesty shall, on or before the first Day of January next, declare, under the Great Seal of Great Britain, that it is expedient that the Lords and Commons of the present Parliament of Great Britain should be the Members of the respective Houses of the first Parliament of the United Kingdom on the Part of Great Britain, then the Lords and Commons or the present Parliament of Great Britain shall accordingly be the Members of the respective Houses of the first Parliament of the United Kingdom on the Part of Great Britain; be it enacted, for and in that Case only; That the present Members of the thirty-two Counties of Ireland, and the two Members for the City of Dublin, and the two Members for the City or Cork, shall be, and they are hereby declared to be, by virtue of this Act, Members for the said Counties and Cities in the first Parliament of the United Kingdom; and that, on a Day and Hour to be appointed by his Majesty under the Great Seal of Ireland, previous to the said first Day of January one thousand eight hundred and one, the Members then serving for the College of the Holy Trinity of Dublin, and for each of the following Cities or Boroughs, that is to say, the City of Waterford, City of Limerick, Borough of Belfast, County and Town of Drogheda, County and Town of Carrickfergus, Borough of Newry, City of Kilkenny, City of Londonderry, Town of Galway, Borough of Clonmell, Town of Wexford, Town of Youghall, Town of Bandon-Bridge, Borough of Armagh, Borough of Dundalk, Town of Kinsale, Borough of Lisburne, Borough of Sligo, Borough of Catherlough, Borough of Ennis, Borough of Dungarvan, Borough of Downpatrick, Borough of Coleraine, Town of Mallow, Borough of Athlone, Town of New Ross, Borough of Tralee, City of Cashel, Borough of Dungannon, Borough of Portarlington, and Borough of Enniskillen, or any five or more of them, shall meet in the now usual Place of Meeting of the House of Commons of Ireland, and the Names of the Members then serving for the said Places and Boroughs, shall be written on separate Pieces of Paper, and the said Papers being folded up, shall be placed in a Glass or Glasses, and shall successively be drawn thereout by the Clerk of the Crown, or his Deputy, who shall then and there attend for that Purpose; and the first drawn Name of a Member of each of the aforesaid Places or Boroughs shall be taken as the Name of the Member to serve for the said Place or Borough in the first Parliament of the United Kingdom; and a Return of the said Names shall be made by the Clerk of the Crown, or his Deputy, to the House of Commons of the first Parliament of the United Kingdom; and a Certificate thereof shall be given respectively by the said Clerk of the Crown, or his Deputy, to each of the Members whose

Names shall have been so drawn: Provided always, That it may be allowed to any Member of any of the said Places or Boroughs, by personal Application, to be then and there made by him to the Clerk of the Crown or his Deputy, or by Declaration in Writing under his Hand, to be transmitted by him to the Clerk of the Crown previous to the said Day so appointed as above, to withdraw his Name previous to the drawing of the Names by Lot; in which Case, of in that of a Vacancy by Death or otherwise of one of the Members of any of the said Places or Boroughs, at the Time of so drawing the Names, the Name of the other Member shall be returned as aforesaid as the Name of the Member to serve for such Place in the first Parliament of the United Kingdom; or if both Members for any such Place or Borough shall so withdraw their Names, or if there shall be a Vacancy of both Members at the Time aforesaid, the Clerk of the Crown shall certify the same to the House of Commons of the first Parliament of the United Kingdom, and shall also express, in such Return, whether any Writ shall then have issued for the Election of a Member or Members to supply such Vacancy; and if a Writ shall so have issued for the Election of one Member only, such Writ shall be superseded, any Election to be thereafter made thereupon shall be null and of no Effect; and if such Writ shall have issued for the Election of two Members, the said two Members shall be chosen accordingly, and their Names being returned by the Clerk of the Crown to the House of Commons of the Parliament of the United Kingdom, one of the said Names shall then be drawn by Lot, in such Manner and Time as the said House of Commons shall direct; and the person whose Name shall be so drawn, shall be deemed to be the Member to sit for such Place in the first Parliament of the United Kingdom; but if, at the

Time aforesaid no Writ shall have issued to supply such Vacancy, none shall thereafter issue until the same be; ordered by Resolution of the House of Commons of the Parliament of the United Kingdom, as in the Case of any other Vacancy of a Seat in the House of Commons of the Parliament of the United Kingdom. And be it enacted, That whenever his Majesty, his Heirs and Successors, shall, by Proclamation under the Great Seal of the United Kingdom, summon a new Parliament of the United Kingdom of Great Britain and Ireland, the Chancellor, Keeper, or Commissioners of the Great Seal of Ireland, shall cause Writs to be issued to the several Counties, Cities, the College of the Holy Trinity of Dublin, and Boroughs in that Part of the United Kingdom called Ireland, specified in this Act, for the Election of Members to serve in the Parliament of the United Kingdom, according to the Number herein-before set forth; and whenever any Vacancy of a Seat in the House of Commons of the Parliament of the United Kingdom, for any of the said Counties, Cities, or Boroughs, or for the said College of the Holy Trinity of Dublin, shall arise, by Death or otherwise, the Chancellor, Keeper, or Commissioners of the Great Seal, upon such Vacancy being certified to them respectively, by the proper Warrant, shall forthwith cause a Writ to issue for the Election for the Election of a Person to fill up such Vacancy; and such Writs, and the Returns thereon, respectively being returned into the Crown Office in that Part of the United Kingdom called Ireland, shall from thence be transmitted to the Crown Office in that Part of the United Kingdom called England, and be certified to the House of Commons in the same Manner as the like Returns have been usually or shall hereafter be certified; and Copies of the said Writs and Returns, attested by the

Chancellor, Keeper or Commissioners of the Great Seal of Ireland for the Time being, shall be preserved in the Crown Office of Ireland, and shall be Evidence of such Writs and Returns, in case the original Writs and Returns shall be lost;' be it enacted, That the said Act, so herein recited, be taken as a Part of this Act, and be deemed to all Intents and Purposes, incorporated within the same.

III. And be it enacted, That the Great Seal of Ireland may, if his Majesty shall so think fit, after the Union, be used in like Manner as before the Union, except where it is otherwise provided by the foregoing Articles, within that Part of the United Kingdom called Ireland; and that his Majesty may, so long as he shall think fit, continue the Privy Council of Ireland to be his Privy Council for that Part of the United Kingdom called Ireland.

THE ANGLO-IRISH TREATY, 1921

1. Ireland shall have the same constitutional status in the Community of Nations known as the British Empire as the Dominion of Canada, the Commonwealth of Australia, the Dominion of New Zealand, and the Union of South Africa with a Parliament having powers to make laws for the peace, order and good government of Ireland and an Executive responsible to that Parliament, and shall be styled and known as the Irish Free State.

2. Subject to the provisions hereinafter set out the position of the Irish Free State in relation to the Imperial Parliament and Government and otherwise shall be that of the Dominion of Canada, and the law, practice and constitutional usage governing the relationship of the Crown or the representative of the Crown and of the Imperial Parliament to the Dominion of Canada shall govern their relationship to the Irish Free State.

3. The representative of the Crown in Ireland shall be appointed in like manner as the Governor-General of Canada and in accordance with the practice observed in the making of such appointments.

4. The oath to be taken by Members of the Parliament of the Irish Free State shall be in the following form:-
I do solemnly swear true faith and allegiance to the Constitution of the Irish Free State as by law established and that I will be faithful to H.M. King George V., his heirs and successors by law, in virtue of the common citizenship of Ireland with Great Britain and her adherence to and membership of the group of nations

forming the British Commonwealth of Nations.

5. The Irish Free State shall assume liability for the service of the Public Debt of the United Kingdom as existing at the date hereof and towards the payment of War Pensions as existing at that date in such proportion as may be fair and equitable, having regard to any just claim on the part of Ireland by way of set-off or counter-claim, the amount of such sums being determined in default of agreement by the arbitration of one or more independent persons being citizens of the British Empire

6. Until an arrangement has been made between the British and Irish Governments whereby the Irish Free State undertakes her own coastal defence, the defence by sea of Great Britain and Ireland shall be undertaken by His Majesty's Imperial Forces, but this shall not prevent the construction or maintenance by the Government of the Irish Free State of such vessels as are necessary for the protection of the Revenue or the Fisheries. The foregoing provisions of this article shall be reviewed at a conference of Representatives of the British and Irish governments, to be held at the expiration of five years from the date hereof with a view to the undertaking by Ireland of a share in her own coastal defence.

7. The Government of the Irish Free State shall afford to His Majesty's Imperial Forces

(a) In time of peace such harbour and other facilities as are indicated in the Annex hereto, or such other facilities as may from time to time be agreed between the British Government and the Government of the Irish Free State; and

(b) In time of war or of strained relations with a Foreign Power such harbour and other facilities as the British

Government may require for the purposes of such defence as aforesaid.

8. With a view to securing the observance of the principle of international limitation of armaments, if the Government of the Irish Free State establishes and maintains a military defence force, the establishments thereof shall not exceed in size such proportion of the military establishments maintained in Great Britain as that which the population of Ireland bears to the population of Great Britain.

9. The ports of Great Britain and the Irish Free State shall be freely open to the ships of the other country on payment of the customary port and other dues.

10. The Government of the Irish Free State agrees to pay fair compensation on terms not less favourable than those accorded by the Act of 1920 to judges, officials, members of Police Forces and other Public Servants who are discharged by it or who retire in consequence of the change of government effected in pursuance hereof. Provided that this agreement shall not apply to members of the Auxiliary Police Force or to persons recruited in Great Britain for the Royal Irish Constabulary during the two years next preceding the date hereof. The British Government will assume responsibility for such compensation or pensions as may be payable to any of these excepted persons.

11. Until the expiration of one month from the passing of the Act of Parliament for the ratification of this instrument, the powers of the Parliament and the Government of the Irish Free State shall not be exercisable as respects Northern Ireland, and the provisions of the Government of Ireland Act 1920, shall, so far as they relate to Northern

Ireland, remain of full force and effect, and no election shall be held for the return of members to serve in the Parliament of the Irish Free State for constituencies in Northern Ireland, unless a resolution is passed by both Houses of the Parliament of Northern Ireland in favour of the holding of such elections before the end of the said month.

12. If before the expiration of the said month, an address is presented to His Majesty by both Houses of the Parliament of Northern Ireland to that effect, the powers of the Parliament and the Government of the Irish Free State shall no longer extend to Northern Ireland, and the provisions of the Government of Ireland Act, 1920, (including those relating to the Council of Ireland) shall so far as they relate to Northern Ireland, continue to be of full force and effect, and this instrument shall have effect subject to the necessary modifications. Provided that if such an address is so presented a Commission consisting of three persons, one to be appointed by the Government of the Irish Free State, one to be appointed by the Government of Northern Ireland, and one who shall be Chairman to be appointed by the British Government shall determine in accordance with the wishes of the inhabitants, so far as may be compatible with economic and geographic conditions, the boundaries between Northern Ireland and the rest of Ireland, and for the purposes of the Government of Ireland Act, 1920, and of this instrument, the boundary of Northern Ireland shall be such as may be determined by such Commission.

13. For the purpose of the last foregoing article, the powers of the Parliament of Southern Ireland under the Government of Ireland Act, 1920, to elect members of the Council of Ireland shall after the Parliament of

the Irish Free State is constituted be exercised by that Parliament.

14. After the expiration of the said month, if no such address as is mentioned in Article 12 hereof is presented, the Parliament and Government of Northern Ireland shall continue to exercise as respects Northern Ireland the powers conferred on them by the Government of Ireland Act, 1920, but the Parliament and Government of the Irish Free State shall in Northern Ireland have in relation to matters in respect of which the Parliament of Northern Ireland has not power to make laws under the Act (including matters which under the said Act are within the jurisdiction of the Council of Ireland) the same powers as in the rest of Ireland, subject to such other provisions as may be agreed in manner hereinafter appearing.

15. At any time after the date hereof the Government of Northern Ireland and the provisional Government of Southern Ireland hereinafter constituted may meet for the purpose of discussing the provisions subject to which the last foregoing Article is to operate in the event of no such address as is therein mentioned being presented and those provisions may include:-

(a) Safeguards with regard to patronage in Northern Ireland.

(b) Safeguards with regard to the collection of revenue in Northern Ireland.

(c) Safeguards with regard to import and export duties affecting the trade or industry of Northern Ireland.

(d) Safeguards for minorities in Northern Ireland.

(e) The settlement of the financial relations between Northern Ireland and the Irish Free State.

(f) The establishment and powers of a local militia in Northern Ireland and the relation of the Defence Forces of the Irish Free State and of Northern Ireland respectively, and if at any such meeting provisions are agreed to, the same shall have effect as if they were included amongst the provisions subject to which the powers of the Parliament and the Government of the Irish Free State are to be exercisable in Northern Ireland under Article 14 hereof. 16. Neither the Parliament of the Irish Free State nor the Parliament of Northern Ireland shall make any law so as either directly or indirectly to endow any religion or prohibit or restrict the free exercise thereof or give any preference or impose any disability on account of religious belief or religious status or affect prejudicially the right of any child to attend a school receiving public money without attending the religious instruction at the school or make any discrimination as respects State aid between schools under the management of different religious denominations or divert from any religious denomination or any educational institution any of its property except for public utility purposes and on payment of compensation.

17. By way of provisional arrangement for the administration of Southern Ireland during the interval which must elapse between the date hereof and the constitution of a Parliament and Government of the Irish Free State in accordance therewith, steps shall be taken forthwith for summoning a meeting of members of Parliament elected for constituencies in Southern Ireland since the passing of the Government of Ireland Act, 1920, and for constituting a provisional Government,

and the British Government shall take the steps necessary to transfer to such provisional Government the powers and machinery requisite for the discharge of its duties, provided that every member of such provisional Government shall have signified in writing his or her acceptance of this instrument. But this arrangement shall not continue in force beyond the expiration of twelve months from the date hereof.

18. This instrument shall be submitted forthwith by His Majesty's Government for the approval of Parliament and by the Irish signatories to a meeting summoned for the purpose of the members elected to sit in the House of Commons of Southern Ireland and if approved shall be ratified by the necessary legislation.

Annex

1. The following are the specific facilities required:- Dockyard Port at Berehaven.

(a) Admiralty property and rights to be retained as at the date hereof. Harbour defences to remain in charge of British care and maintenance parties. Queenstown.

(b) Harbour defences to remain in charge of British care and maintenance parties. Certain mooring buoys to be retained for use of His Majesty's ships. Belfast Lough.

(c) Harbour defences to remain in charge of British care and maintenance parties. Lough Swilly.

(d) Harbour defences to remain in charge of British care and maintenance parties. AVIATION.

(e) Facilities in the neighbourhood of the above ports for

coastal defence by air. OIL FUEL STORAGE.

(f) Haulbowline [and] Rathmullen[:] To be offered for sale to commercial companies under guarantee that purchasers shall maintain a certain minimum stock for Admiralty purposes.

2. A Convention shall be made between the British Government and the Government of the Irish Free State to give effect to the following conditions :-

(a) That submarine cables shall not be landed or wireless stations for communication with places outside Ireland be established except by agreement with the British Government; that the existing cable landing rights and wireless concessions shall not be withdrawn except by agreement with the British Government; and that the British Government shall be entitled to land additional submarine cables or establish additional wireless stations for communication with places outside Ireland.

(b) That lighthouses, buoys, beacons, and any navigational marks or navigational aids shall be maintained by the Government of the Irish Free State as at the date hereof and shall not be removed or added to except by agreement with the British Government.

(c) That war signal stations shall be closed down and left in charge of care and maintenance parties, the Government of the Irish Free State being offered the option of taking them over and working them for commercial purposes subject to Admiralty inspection, and guaranteeing the upkeep of existing telegraphic communication therewith.

3. A Convention shall be made between the same Governments for the regulation of Civil Communication by Air.

Other Works Published by the East India Publishing Company

The Philippics
Cicero

On the Duty of Civil Disobedience
Henry David Thoreau

Socialism
John Stuart Mill

Communist Manifesto
Karl Marx & Friedrich Engles

The Prince
Niccolo Machiavelli

The Republic
Plato

The Age of Reason
Thomas Paine

The Art of War
Sun Tzu

Will to Power
Friedrich Nietzsche

Meditations
Marcus Aurelius

www.eastindiapublishing.com

Printed in Great Britain
by Amazon